Numbers

Understand the Math and Science of Numerology,
Zodiac Signs, Horoscopes, Star Signs and Chakras
to Interpreting Love, Family, Career

(Spiritual Guide to Raise Your Consciousness)

Heather Bunker

Published by Rob Miles

© **Heather Bunker**

All Rights Reserved

Numbers: Understand the Math and Science of Numerology, Zodiac Signs, Horoscopes, Star Signs and Chakras to Interpreting Love, Family, Career (Spiritual Guide to Raise Your Consciousness)

ISBN 978-1-989990-45-2

All rights reserved. No part of this guide may be reproduced in any form without permission in writing from the publisher except in the case of brief quotations embodied in critical articles or reviews.

Legal & Disclaimer

The information contained in this book is not designed to replace or take the place of any form of medicine or professional medical advice. The information in this book has been provided for educational and entertainment purposes only.

The information contained in this book has been compiled from sources deemed reliable, and it is accurate to the best of the Author's knowledge; however, the Author cannot guarantee its accuracy and validity and cannot be held liable for any errors or omissions. Changes are periodically made to this book. You must consult your doctor or get professional medical advice before using any of the suggested remedies, techniques, or information in this book.

Upon using the information contained in this book, you agree to hold harmless the Author from and against any damages, costs, and expenses, including any legal fees potentially resulting from the application of any of the information provided by this guide. This disclaimer applies to any damages or injury caused by the use and application, whether directly or indirectly, of any advice or information presented, whether for breach of contract, tort, negligence, personal injury, criminal intent, or under any other cause of action.

You agree to accept all risks of using the information presented inside this book. You need to consult a professional medical practitioner in order to ensure you are both able and healthy enough to participate in this program.

Table of Contents

INTRODUCTION 1

CHAPTER 1: SUN (NUMBER – 1) 8

CHAPTER 2: NUMEROLOGY 101 15

CHAPTER 3: WHAT IS NUMEROLOGY? 24

CHAPTER 4: HOW EASY IS IT TO UNDERSTAND NUMEROLOGY? 33

CHAPTER 5: THE HISTORY OF NUMEROLOGY 40

CHAPTER 6: HOW TO IDENTIFY THE NUMBERS TO USE IN NUMEROLOGY 45

CHAPTER 7: PERIODICITY AND ALLOCATION OF NUMBERS 50

CHAPTER 8: IF YOU BORN ON THE 3. (THIRD) OR 12TH (TWELFTH), OR 21ST (TWENTY FIRST) OR 30TH (THIRTIETH) OF ANY MONTH THAN KINDLY READ THE FOLLOWING: .. 61

CHAPTER 9: HOW TO WORK OUT YOUR NUMEROLOGY NUMBERS 73

CHAPTER 10: THE DESTINY NUMBER 80

CHAPTER 11: CALCULATING YOUR LIFE PATH 90

CHAPTER 12: CARETAKER AND GIVER; THE PUBLIC RELATIONS EXPERT 102

CHAPTER 13: THE ZODIAC 118

CHAPTER 14: PERSONAL DAY 136

CHAPTER 15: PERSONALITY NUMBER 143

CHAPTER 16: WHAT ABOUT CHANGED NAMES 162

CHAPTER 17: BREAKING DOWN THE EXPRESSION NUMBER FURTHER 165

CHAPTER 18: SIX OF WANDS 168

CHAPTER 19: THE COSMIC CLOCK OF SCORPIO 195

CONCLUSION 206

Introduction

What do this numbers signifies?

The first set of numbers is Mr. Donald Trump's (US President) birth date

The second set of numbers is Mr.Xi Jin Ping's (Chinese President) birth date

US PRESIDENT Mr. Donald Trump and Chinese President Mr. Xin Jin Pin can celebrate their birthdays together, since both are born in the month of June one day apart, the former on the 14 and the latter on the 15 but they are at logger heads

In numerology, the science of numbers 13, 14, 16 and 19 bear karmic debt, which means they owe and have an emotional baggage linked to their past lives. Like it or not and believe it or not, numbers surrounds us daily from the time we enter this world, until our last exhalation. In a family the number of people is calculated for social security and parents long to count their first born baby's first footsteps. In school the marks you secure are numbers and each birth date is celebrated with pump and gaiety. In contrast each death date is remembered in sorrow albeit poignantly.

The Roman numerals from 1 to 9 are important in numerology and the constant zero. The Babylonians gave us the magical number 60 on which time is based, like sixty seconds and sixty minutes, which when extrapolated give s us 1440 minutes in a day, 86400 seconds in a day and 31536000 seconds in a year. In the commercial world, the stock market relies on numbers and for an athlete to monetize his/her name depends on the medals won in the international sporting arena. All elements of life inevitably, intimately and intricately are connected in variably to a single number or an amalgamation or a combination of numerals.

This book aims to give a comprehensive, incisive and concise view of the different facets in numerology not compromising on its finer points and nuances. Numerology has its genesis in the great philosopher, Pythagoras and the Indian Vedic science. Pythagoras theorem is an integral part of mathematics and Physics and that he was the first proponent of vegetarianism and transmigration of the soul is a lesson known fact.

People mistakenly cry over their bad luck and miss-fortune, when their life partners go away or when they cannot get their desired and deserved promotions not knowing all these depend on their life paths, their names and their name synchronization. All these are linked to numbers.

You see! I have a sibling, who has a toxic relationship with me, as his life path and mine clash and there is no congruity. In contrast my last sibling is close and helpful because his life path and mine is the same number which happens to be life path number 5.

In some relationships, when their life path numbers are not in sync, their relationship will only progress to a semi-circle and not to a full circle. They will probably be waiting for a God –send miracle to salvage it.

Have you wondered, why in your office you are more close to someone and then with one of your family member. You select a particular person to be your confidante? Or, as it has happened to me several times. When at a party you start to gaze at a particular unknown face. As though you know that person. Strange but un-doubtedly true. That is because both your life paths (which I will discuss subsequently) could be on the same level and you feel a common magnetic attraction though it is the first time you are seeing that person. Your name too has that inherent power value to ignite and propel your destiny. Ever wondered with a logical answer, why you are well liked even though you are a recalcitrant rascal among a group of friends? It is because your name or life path is in agreement to the rest. Ever seen workers coming into work late and getting off without even a warning and students ending in assignments overdue, without any punitive actions taken on them.. All these has to do with numerology.

Case in Point: our Gregorian calendar adopted in 1582, begins with the birth of Christ (Anno Domini). Our current calendar takes its base the year Jesus Christ was born, Which is 25 December 0000, which gives Jesus 2+5=7 as his Psychic number(Psychic number discussed in detail in Chapter), according to Pythagoras the number 7 is the most complete and the most religious of all the numbers and 2+5+1+2 gives us=10. Which makes him a leader (See Life Path 1-Page no) because his life path is 1.

Let us look into the birth date of Prophet Mohammed and his birth date is 22 April 571. His birth date 22 is an amazing master number. (See master number 22 in Chapter and page no.), his birth date contains the power of double 2s. now number 2 is the sign of a master mind and the double 2s amplifies his cognitive operations two-fold and 2+2 gives us 4 and this number signifies that he is a naturally industrious and hardworking (this can be gleaned from the time he worked for Khatija, first wife and how he impressed her with his industrious nature). the life path of the Prophet is 21, which when reduced is becomes 2+1=3 and the two numbers (2 and 1) shows a continuation of the qualities of the number 2, which is that of master mind and 1 which shows his leadership qualities, the traits of which he illustrate in the various battles and even as the first caliph of Madeena/Bhagdad and as a number 3 he exuded creativity, kindness and empathy in many instances.

In brief this book shall be an eye opener for the beginner and hone the skills of a mediocre Numerology-aficionado and an unavoidable mecca to circumambulate for professionals and nascent numerologists who expire to eke out a living.

Chapter 1: Sun (Number – 1)

People who are born under the dates 1, 10, 19 or 28 or the date total by adding all the digits of the date to single number which becomes 1 or as per numerology if the name total gives sum 1 are coming under SUN power.

Number 1 indicates Sun and it gives life to the entire world. Either the date is giving total of 1 or as per numerology if the name gives number 1 (means 1, 10, 19 and 28), these people are on top of everything. They are able to lead a team or party or even the nation and all the ruling qualities are applicable for them in all the ways.

They are able to shine in politics very well. Also hard working, open speaking, helping in nature, completing anything on time, friendliness, prestigious life, business ability, artily minded, respecting others are good qualities.

Generally they don't disturb and trouble others. Though, if these people are bold, straight forward & courageous; few times they are defeated if the sun power is low. Basically they are affected by many eye problems and blood pressure.

People born under 1: They are fast, shouting in nature, not getting adjusted in any situation, believing in everything and willing to work hard.

People born under 10: Bit slow in nature, keeping the secret safe, good friendship, getting fame, becoming famous and shows love and affection with others.

People born under 19: Excellent mind power, quite in nature but able to fight for their benefits, never changing their mind for anything except their decisions and good writing abilities.

People born under 28: Smart and good looking people, believing everything, being cheated by others and sometimes being as a joker.

Names and Number 1:

You will be ruled by SUN or the number 1 if you have the name total as 1 by adding up all the alphabets numbers making a single digit. (Example: **RAJEI** = 2+1+1+5+1 = 10).

But, remember that the people born under 1, 4 or 8 (either the date or sum of date digits) only can have names under 1. Then only it will give good results. For others it may give trouble and lot of failures in life.

So, check the numbers and alphabets in the introduction chapter and find your name digits or sum accordingly. If not lucky, change letters or names to good numbers as said above.

Good and Bad Numbers Under 1 (for names by adding all the alphabets' digits)
1 – Single letter name is not considered like A, I, J etc.. So let us ignore this 1 for name.

10 – Good monitory benefits always. Also life goes with 50 – 50 chances. One time there will be up trend and another time will go down obviously. Every work will be considered and watched by others; so discipline and honesty are necessary.

19 – Excellent attractive number and the name in this number is equivalent to kingdom and there will be continuous victory, fame, happiness, prosperity, abundance etc. Always looks like young people and they are powerful. Sun shines always in life and gives open minded and straight forward characters.

28 – Moves to top with hard work and suddenly comes down to starting point again. Not so good number as the sun power is low. Sometimes people under this number may loose entire wealth and properties.

37 – Good for ordinary people to go up in life. Every day is a treasure in life and this number keeps on top by giving gradual growth. Male and female attraction, help, monitory benefits are possible much. If people are already rich & in high status then they have to be satisfied with whatever they have. Else it will automatically put them down if they create unnecessary problems to others.

46 – People having this number by adding their name alphabets, they have to be honest. It will give king or kingdom status in every business or work or any other area. Need to use intelligence, wisdom and knowledge and grow in life with fame and wealth.

55 – Create, maintain and destroy number and people under this number always win their enemies. Gives more inner strength and super knowledge than others to be on the victory side. Cures diseases too!

64 – Gives mind, body and soul power. Can do wonders to become world famous. Mind reading is possible. Many rewards in one or more field might be true. Political or government status will be number one. Others may obey these people naturally.

73 – Generally good number and gives all the necessary things more than we need in our life. Daily success and quick growth in a short span possible. To be honest, they have to believe in god.

82 – Gives angelic powers to people. May get siddhi powers by god's grace. But, able to get all the properties like jewels, grains, ruling areas etc.

91 – Good for travel success. Business will grow automatically. Victory in everything is possible.

100 – Not so good number under SUN.

10

Lucky Days: 1, 10 & 19 are good. (Either day or sum of the digits in date).28 is unlucky number as described before.

Important Days: 4, 13, 22 and 31. But good luck will work out automatically. Don't start any new task these days.

Unlucky Days: 8, 17 and 26. Avoid all the good start-ups or do not start anything in life in these days.

Work/Business: Only divine related business like yoga, astrology, art/music, sculpture etc are good. Else these people must work under government or politics or in any industry etc.

Can join people at work or business with 1,3,4,5 and avoid 2 & 7 people.

Marriage/ Life Partner: People under 1 may choose 2, 4, 5 and 8 people as their life partners. 3 and 6 people are also good for them.

Lucky Colours: Yellow and Red.

Lucky Metal: **Gold.**

Lucky Stone: Ruby and Yellow Sapphire.

Personalities Under Number 1:

LENIN – 10-4-1870 (1 & 3)

MARTIN LUTHER – 10-11-1483 (1 & 1)

JAMES WATT – 19-01-1736 (1 & 1)

BILL GATES – 28-10-1955 (1 & 4)

Chapter 2: Numerology 101

This is an extremely important chapter since you will be able to understand what numerology is all about and will be able to grasp the essence of numerology.

What is numerology?

Numerology has the word 'numero' which means numbers. This goes to say that numerology is a science or a system that helps you gain knowledge and information about yourself and the people in your universe by using these numbers as the symbols.

Ancient Chaldeans were the ones who had deciphered that every entity was made up of energy, which would vibrate at a state that varied from the next entity. This is a concept that modern science is only catching up to now! The Chaldeans had immense knowledge about the laws of correspondence and they always found a way to explain any phenomenon using the first 9 digits of the number system.

Numbers have always been perceived as archetypes or gestalts that are found within every entity. These archetypes have the ability to transfer the energy that is buried deep within you into the world. This is a principle that has existed for decades and is proven to be true when there is a consciousness around. These numbers are not only what we use for counting but can also be used to separate chaos and order in the universe.

It is never difficult to understand the mystical images and systems that are used in astrology or even understand the images that are found on the Tarot. But, it is extremely difficult to associate a number or an alphabet with a certain meaning or attribute since they are used very often in order to communicate. Most people find it extremely difficult to understand that numbers can have any use apart from being used as measurements or even to estimate the quantities since that is how they are used every single day!

Why is it called Numerology?

The study of numbers to understand the destiny of a person was only called Numerology in the year 1937 by Dr. Julia Seton. It was referred to as divination, Arithmancy, or even Kabbalah. If you are someone who is a fan of Harry Potter, you will realize that in the book, 'Prisoner of Azkaban', Hermione takes a subject called Arithmancy that deals with the study of numbers!

There are different schools of numerology that have originated from Taoism and follow the Chinese schools of thought — Yin and Yang and the Five Elements. There is a belief that these methods are much older than what they have developed to in Japan — 9 Ki or Kyusei — and China — Yijing or I-Ching. The most popular Chinese system of Astrology, which is called the Four Pillars, is a method of numerology that is built on a calendar instead of dealing with the movement of the stars and the planets.

There are numerous methods in India where astrology is based on certain numerological techniques that are dependent on certain magical squares and harmonics. These are only based on the approximate positions of the planets or the formation of the zodiac in the skies. They are majorly the forms or sequences of the cycles of time and do not depend only on the positions of the planets. They are mostly based on the values of the numbers and the vibrations behind these numbers.

History of Numerology

It is always good to understand how numerology came into existence before you delve into understanding and analyzing numbers. Unfortunately, the history is cloudy and vague and there is no evidence of where numerology had first started. A majority of numerologists believe that the earliest records of numerology were found in Egypt and in Babylon. The Chaldean system was born and developed in these records with the influence of Hebrew. There is evidence that numerology was used thousands of years ago in Rome, Japan, Greece and China. The credit of modern numerology has gone to the Greek philosopher, Pythagoras.

Pythagoras is an age-old philosopher and most of us know who he is because we were taught his theories in a mathematics class as children in school. He was born in Greece in the year 590BC and was the best philosopher of his day. He is an extremely important person in the development of mathematics. Sadly, very little is known about him and his achievements. There is very little information about his childhood, but people claim that he was a charismatic and attractive man and was loved by everyone around him. It has been claimed that he was an athlete and had won many awards at the Olympic Games held at Greece.

It was when he was fifty that Pythagoras decided to establish a school that was more like a secret society in Italy. He called the school the semi – circle and taught both men and women more about mathematics, music and astronomy. The students of the school were sworn to secrecy and were implored to never put any of his teachings into writing ever. The students had to remain silent for five years in order to ensure that they have faith and also reach a level of contemplation that goes deeper between the layers. The information that is available about Pythagoras has only been obtained after his death.

Pythagoras never tried to solve problems in mathematics but tried to understand the theory and principles that existed in mathematics. He always tried to dig deeper to understand the concepts of mathematics. He had the belief that he could express every entity or occurrence in the universe using numbers and also tried to create a system that was explained to the world by different Greek philosophers. Pythagoras was not the person who had created numerology, but it was because of his theories that the system of numerology exists. It is for this reason that he is often called the Father of Numerology. It is Julia Seton who had coined the term numerology and has also spread the awareness about numerology in modern times and in different parts of the world.

Although numerology is a system or a science that is the least understood, it has gained immense popularity in the last few decades due to the fact that this system has been used to understand and discover the secret meanings of life and to predict the future.

What are the three facets of numerology?

It has been said that numerology has only three facets that are exceedingly important. The first facet is Numerology is the study of numbers that have vibrations whose patterns have been rooted deeply into the order of the universe. The second facet is Arithmancy, which has been discovered by the author of the Harry potter series J. K. Rowling. This facet depends on the numbers and identified the different techniques that are used to manipulate the numbers and extract their meaning based on their different relationships. You will find that you are able to obtain the information that you are seeking when you understand Arithmancy better. The last facet is called Isopsephy or Gematria in Greek or Aramaic or Hebrew respectively. This facet uses different techniques to associate an alphabet or the phenomena of the alphabet of any language to a number! These methods will ensure that you can convert every name and word into a pattern of numeric symbols.

You will find that none of the facets can operate without the other since each of the facets form one leg of the tripod that balances Numerology. Through numerology you will be able to understand

and examine your inner nature and will be able to look at different processes – physical, spiritual and psychological – which enhance your experiences in the world. You will be able to understand what it is that makes you who you are and will also help you identify the path you should undertake in order to navigate through the events in your life.

Through numerology you will be able to understand your strengths and also overcome any weakness that you may have. The truth is that any information that you want to know can be found easily if you understand the patterns of the numbers and their vibrations.

Chapter 3: What Is Numerology?

Numerology is the study of numbers and their mystical relationships with coinciding life events or circumstances. It is a belief associated with astrology and paranormal events because science has never been able to establish a justifiable relationship between numbers and the events being associated to the numbers. Nevertheless, numerology exists in modern science and is known as pseudoscience or pseudomathematics.

A numerologist is any person who has faith in numerical patterns whether he/she practices traditional numerology.

History of Numerology

The Greek mathematician, Pythagoras (564 – 470 B.C), is believed to be the father and originator of numerology. He and other philosophers of his time believed that there was greater actuality in mathematical concepts as compared to physical ones because mathematical concepts were easier to classify and regulate hence more practical. St Augustine of Hippo who lived between 354 and 430 A.D also believed that every occurrence in life has a numerical relationship and that it's for the mind to investigate and unravel these relationships or seek divine grace for interpretation. He wrote in his literary discourse that, "Numbers have been offered to humans by the deity as the universal language to help confirm the truth".

Following the first council of Nicaea in 325 A.D, departures from the state church's beliefs were considered law violations in the Roman Empire. Christian authorities of that time were not in support of numerology as they ended up categorizing it with magic, astrology and other kinds of divination, under unapproved beliefs. Despite this opposition, though, numerology's spiritual significance did not disappear. Several numbers, including the 'Jesus Number' have been analyzed and commented by **Dorotheus of Gaza** and numerology is still used in conservative Greek Orthodox circles at least. Numerology is widely covered in Sir Thomas Browne's **The Garden of Cyrus** (1658) where he, throughout the book, tries to demonstrate how the Quincunx pattern's relationship with the number five can be found in design, arts and nature, particularly botany.

There are various antecedents connected to modern numerology. According to Ruth Drayer's **Numerology, the Power in Numbers,** between 1800 and 1900 A.D, Mrs. Dow Balliett connected Pythagoras' theory with Biblical reference. In 1972, Dr, Juno Jordan, Balliett's student, further modified numerology to make it the system it is today – Pythagorean'. It is important to note that the title Pythagorean' has nothing to do with Pythagoras' contribution towards the system.

In Juno Jordan's book, **The Romance in Your Name,** he explains the system for determining key numerological influences' in the birth date and name of an individual, which are still used today. The use of numerology to assess events or personality was further expanded on by subsequent numerologists/numerology experts such as Florence Campbell, Lynn Buess, Mark Gruner and Kathleen Roquemore. The different schools of numerology, which the above numerologists belong to, offer various meanings of basic digits, definitions that sometimes conflict.

Methods of Numerology

Alphabetic Systems

Alphabetic letters have been assigned numerical value in a number of numerology systems including Greek numerals, Armenian numerals, Hebrew numerals and Arabic Abjad numerals. Here is an example of how numbers can be assigned to letters:

1 = a, j, s

2 = b, k, t

3 = c, l, u

4 = d, m, v

5 = e, n, w

6 = f, o, x

7 = g, p, y

8 = h, q, z

9 = i, r

They are then summed as follows:

For example;

2293 ... 2 + 2 + 9 + 3 = 16 ... 1 + 6 = 7

Come ... 3 + 6 + 4 + 5 = 18 ... 1 + 8 = 9

These examples have been calculated using decimal arithmetic. There exists other number systems such as hexadecimal, binary, octal and vigesimal. Using any of these systems to sum the same digits in the above examples will yield varying results.

Other methods of calculation include Pythagorean, Hebraic, Chaldean, Japanese,

Phonetic, Helyn Hitchcock's method, Indian and Arabic.

Abjad System

Abjad numerals or Abjad notation represent the Arabic numerology system. In this system, each character in the Arabic alphabet has been assigned a numerical value. Ilm-ul-huroof (science of alphabet letters) and ilm-ul-cipher (science of cipher) originate from the Abjad system.

Chinese Numerology

In Chinese numerology, different numbers translate to different meanings and certain number combinations are believed to denote good or bad luck. Commonly, even numbers are considered luckier due to the notion that luck comes in pairs.

Numerology in Science

If the main inspiration for a scientific theory is a set of patterns and not scientific observations, then the theory is labeled numerology'. The term numerology' is very widespread in the scientific world and is commonly used to write off a theory as questionable science'.

A good example of numerology in science is the classification of elements in groups or columns (atomic triads) which led to the discovery of the periodic table. The atomic masses of the lightest and heaviest elements of a group or column were summed up and averaged. The average was found to be very close to the weight of the intermediate element. Although the principle never applied on every triplet in a column or group, it worked on enough settings to allow scientists create generalizations.

Generally, the coincidental similarity of certain large numbers - as realizeed by the likes of physicist Paul Dirac, astronomer Arthur Stanley Eddington and mathematician Hermann Weyl — is the mother of such breakthroughs as the discovery of the atomic triads. Even James G. Gilson's "Quantum Theory of Gravity" was majorly based on Dirac's hypothesis of large number coincidence.

Skepticism

According to skeptics, numbers have no connection with life events and circumstances, and cannot influence a person's life by themselves. They base their argument on the belief that there is no evidence to back numerologists' claims. For instance, there is no proof that all people born on, say, March 31st have similar futures or fates as numerologists claim.

Regarding this, two known studies have been conducted to date – one in 1993 in the UK and one in Israel in 2012 – both of them yielding negative results. The one conducted in Israel was more famous and it included a numerologist by profession, and 200 participants. Negative results were produced even after having the experiment repeated twice.

Even with this opposition from scientists and religious leaders, numerologists still has a very good percentage of people in the world who believe numerology because it has either worked on them or someone they know. You can not exactly tell whether the events and experiences you encounter are a result of the use of numerology and numbers or mere circumstances. But, with the many cases of people who have come out to testify for numerology, its almost beyond doubt that numerology has some - however little - influence on our lives.

Chapter 4: How Easy Is It To Understand Numerology?

Let us begin by saying that anyone anywhere will find something of interest in numerology. Likewise, supposing you feel inclined, you could learn numerology in great depth, including learning how to incorporate vibrations into determining your character. It is said that each item in this wide universe – and they are really many – vibrates at its unique frequency. There are even different energies and also qualities that go with these vibrations; and with deeper knowledge of this discipline that is numerology, you could relate the vibrations to your personality by using your name and birth date.

For now, however, we are keeping it simple. And this is how:

We shall look at the simplest, but very effective way, of applying numerology.

Do you remember from your math class that some numbers were considered simple and others complex? In this regard, some numbers have single digits while others have double and multiple digits. Numerology opts to use the single digits, though it also adds few others that are very simple to handle.

Here are the numbers that determine your stand in numerology:

One (1); Two (2); Three (3); Four (4); Five (5); Six (6); Seven (7); Eight (8); Nine (9); Eleven (11); Twenty-two (22).

Birth Date

The exact date that you were born is said to give us entry to your innermost self. And you are supposed to reduce that date to the simple numbers that numerology utilizes. Those numbers that numerology utilizes are referred to as Master Numbers.

Example:

If you were born on 1st January 1977, you can see below how to deduce that birth date to a usable number.

It is 1+1+1977 = 1979

Aha! But the resultant number is still complex. From here then, you proceed to simplify it further.

You get 1+9+7+9 = 26

Aha! The result is simpler but still not simple enough for numerological application. So take the simplification further.

2+6 = 8

The significance of the resultant number 8 is that it is the one that shows the qualities that broadly define you; and that is in broad terms. You need to realize that you have been born with certain potential, but it is up to you to do things and utilize opportunities that maximize that potential.

That is the reason there are other people who are also Eights just like you, yet when you screen them, they do not seem to perform like you do. But if you are close to them, you will appreciate their potential. Where they seem to doubt themselves, they would not succumb to self-doubt or environmental pressure, if only they knew what their potential was. And that is mostly why numerology is very important. It gives you courage to pursue your goals even when nobody else has much faith in you.

For that reason, the digit that results from the master numbers of your birth date (day, month and year) is referred to as your Life Path Number.

It not only determines the direction that your life takes, but also its momentum. That is why some people are great in leadership and other things and those qualities show up late in life, while others have different qualities that show up very early in life.

What happens when you have the numbers 11 or 22 in your birth date?

Easy: you appreciate that those two numbers, 11 and 22, are already master numbers, though they are double digits. So, you leave them unchanged.

Example:

Your birth date is 22nd November 1977

The day does not change; it remains 22.

The month does not change; it remains 11

What changes is the year: 1+9+7+7 = 24; 2+4 = 6

So, the next step is to add up 22+11+6 = 39; 3+9 = 12; 1+2 = 3

Your Life Path number is, therefore, 3.

What, then, after getting the Life Path Numbers?

These Life Path numbers are quite loaded. They bear the qualities and tendencies that mark your life. Each of the Life Path numbers is unique, and as you will bear witness, no single person is the same in character; mannerisms; and in all levels of success in every sphere. There must be a variation here or there.

But many of us fall on the same Life Path number – there, very likely, lays your confusion. And it is understandable. But you need to know that your Life Path number is an indicator of your potential and your core qualities. A lot more can happen within your environment that may blur some of those attributes. The great thing about knowing your Life Path number in advance is that you can deliberately work towards achieving that which you have potential for. Being sure of your potential gives you motivation to pursue the relevant goals without wavering, and abandoning those that clearly go against the grain.

Core numbers in numerology

We have dealt with your Life Path number, and if you decide to delve further into this interesting topic of numerology, you will see how the other core numbers work. The other core numbers include:

- The Expression number
- The Personality number
- The Heart's Desire number
- The Birthday number

Chapter 5: The History Of Numerology

It's time to talk about the history of numerology. Knowing the history will allow us to really understand and be able to help you really get a feeling for what this is. You do need to know the history, not just because it is interesting, but it can also help you really understand just what it is you're getting into, and some of the various factors that come about.

The first thing that you have to know was the founder of modern numerology was actually Pythagoras, who was a Greek mathematician that lived from 569-470 B.C. He is said to be the one who was the starter of what we call numerology today. He believed that many of the mathematical concepts were more practical than the physical ones out there, and they had a greater actuality. There was another philosopher at the time who also spoke on this named St. Augustine of Hippo, who also stated that numbers were also the language that the deities would use to confer to humans in terms of the truths that are out there. Hippo also believed that everything in life had a numerical relationship, but the only way to see it, was to actually have the desire to seek out and look at the secrets of the various relationships and have them seen through divine grace. You can also see numerology in many early Christian texts as well.

However, in 325 A.D, it was soon see that the beliefs of the state church were actually violations of the church within the Roman Empire. The concept of numerology hadn't been favorable by the Christian authority, and soon it was considered unapproved beliefs along with astrology and even divination and magic. However, even with this purging of these concepts, there were still some other numerology elements that still stuck around. Items such as "sacred" numbers, and even the Jesus number had been allowed to look at. However, even with it, there were still arguments that there was use for it. You can see this in the bible, since the numbers 3 and 7 have great spiritual significance in the bible. You can see it in the seven days of creation, and even in the 3 times that Jesus asked god if he could avoid the crucifixion and the fact that he was crucified at 3 in the afternoon. Also, the number eight does also have a symbol of change as well, and these numbers were often seen in many of the major Christian texts out there.

There were also some alchemical theories that were closely related to numerology, for example with experiments that have numerology in them that is based on the Arabic names of the substances. You can see this later on in Sir Thomas Browne's discourse as well, where the author talks about how the number five can be found throughout life, and even in botany and in the arts.

However, numerology did have some ties back to before the Greeks, and they should be noted. The actual origins are before Pythagoras, and it can be seen actually in the Hebrew kabbalah. In the twentieth century, you ten start to see this discipline come up once again in some books that are published between 1911-1917 by L. Dow Balliet. This helped the art of numerology continue on, along with Florence Campbell, and within the next few decades, there was more literature on the subject than ever before to people.

Numerology did widely evolve over the last 90 years, and it has become a lot more popular as of late. However, it is also known for a long time, so it might've just been hiding from us. However, numerology is a common study today, and it

There is some skepticism in this, because many of the skeptics do argue that there is no occult ties to numbers and there isn't' a significance that these numbers can influence a person's life. However, the numbers are seen as more of a superstition and a pseudoscience by these people. There are experiments going on, and most of the time they have produced negative results. However, it's still a popular subject, and it's one that has been around for so long that you might not even realize it.

Numerology is a study that's been around for what has seen to be forever. It's one that has a lot of rich history, and through that, you'll be able to really see just where this can take it. It's different from the usual studies out there nowadays, but you will learn a whole lot about it in the ensuing chapters. Numerology is interesting, and you will soon be able to dive into it even more so

Chapter 6: How To Identify The Numbers To Use In Numerology

How many numbers could you write in sequence given time and writing material? Well, you really cannot mention the number, because in reality, the possible number count is infinite. Beginning from ones to tens to hundreds to thousands to trillions – well, you just cannot get an end to the count. For that reason, the experts behind numerology have come up with a way of keeping the numbers simple.

Here is how you get your numbers:

All numbers need to be reduced to single digits before their meaning can be established. That is one reason that makes numerology easy to apply. In addition to keeping calculations simple, there is also need to identify numbers according to relevance. In short, what are you seeking to understand at this particular time? Is it something to do with your character, matters relating to your past or matters of an entirely different nature? To understand this analysis, you need to know what kinds of numbers you have as options.

Here are the most important numbers:

Life Path Number

The Expression number

The Personality number

The Heart's Desire number

The Birthday number

Life Path Number

From your birth date you derive a simple digit that gives you insight into what you are all about, which is what your life path is. What this effectively means is that just from your date of birth you can tell what your potential in life is. You can also tell how inspired or laid back you are; and this is the information you need in order to know where to put more effort and resources and which sphere of life to adjust.

In simple terms, numerology, through this core number, can help you in making major life decisions. For example, you may get information that underlines your suitability as a medic as opposed to a policeman; or even a career person as opposed to a business person. Making decisions that suit your life not only saves you future heartaches but also ensures your resources are well utilized. Many are the teenagers who, for example, invest in college education only to abandon the course halfway when they realize that it is not their thing.

How to reduce your Birth Date into a single digit:

Supposing your date and month of birth, the date that shows what your zodiac sign is, is July 18th and the year is 2015. You need to add all the individual numbers involved until such a time as you have only a single digit. And in our particular case:

18+7+2015 = 2040

Wow! That's huge! But it is alright because you have the opportunity to now add the individual digits that make up 2040.

2+0+4+0 = 6

Great! Are you not home and dry now? Right there you have established what your life path number is; and it is 6.

You are now ready to acquire the information you need regarding your path in life because you know where to look – under Number 6. The reason you can have someone else falling under this same number and you end up doing better in life is that information is power. And once you know what weaknesses you have you can be proactive in adjusting; and as far as your potential goes, you can do something to enhance what you are already doing right.

Importance of the single digits

The numbers you end up using in numerology are referred to as Master

Numbers. They are the single digits that you look up when you want to understand what you are predisposed to in life. Of course, single digits range from 1 – 9. However, you need to consider the fact that the number 11 comprises two master numbers. The same case with 22; numbers that are, in fact, of importance in astrology too. So these numbers are to be left exactly as they are as proceed with your reading as numerology provides for them.

Clarification of Master Numbers as either Feminine or Masculine

Masculine or feminine...? Well, numerology is nothing like biology and so you can be sure this has nothing to do with whether a number is male or female – it cannot be either, anyway. What the two attributes of femininity and masculinity allude to are the characteristics associated with the individual numbers. Are the bearers of those life path numbers geared towards having tough traits or soft ones? Tough traits, of course, are linked to masculinity while the soft ones are linked to femininity. That is generally the case as you will soon see.

Chapter 7: Periodicity And Allocation Of Numbers

DIFFERENT DATES OF BIRTH AND PERIODS

A date of birth can consist of:

6 numbers e.g. 2. 2. 1972

or

7 numbers e.g. 2. 12. 1972

or

8 numbers e.g. 12. 12. 1972

MAJOR PERIODS

All the above three types of dates of birth will have a **Major Period of 9 years.** This is as follows:

0 to 9 9 to 18 18 to 27 27 to 36 36 to 45 45 to 54 54 to 63 63 to 72 and so on.

The above number periods indicate ages.

When we say 0 to 9 years, it means from birth to 9 years of age. So also, 9 to 18 years means from age 9 till 18 years of age.

0 to 9	9 to 18	18 to 27	27 to 36	36 to 45	45 to 54	54 to 63	63 to 72
4	1	1	9	8	6	4	1

Example: For a date of birth 2.1.1970, the period 0 to 9 years shall be interpreted as from 2.1.1970 till the midnight of 2.1.1979. Because, after midnight, the date will change to 3. This means age 9 is completed and the next age group of 9 to 18 years will begin.

Similarly, 9 to 18 years will mean from the midnight of 2.1.1979 till the midnight of 2.1.1988.

MAJOR PERIODS AND ALLOCATED NUMBERS

Now, to each of the above 9-year periods or cycles, we have to allocate numbers from the date of birth.

Example: Date of birth: 4.1.1986. Major period = 9 years each.

So, we have

As can be seen above, **numbers are allotted to the periods from the date of birth in a serial order.** As numbers are allotted in a serial order, the first number in the date of birth, which is 4, repeats after the age of 54, followed by the rest of the numbers.

Henceforth, all these numbers will be referred to as **allotted numbers.**

What do these allotted numbers indicate?

Looking at the above date of birth, it means that from birth to 9 years of age, the number 4 will have influence.

From 9 to 18 years, the number 1 will have influence.

From 45 to 54 years, the number 6 will have influence.

PERIODICITY DURATION

	A **6 NUMBERS** (e.g. 2.2.1972)	B **7 NUMBERS** (e.g. 2.12.1972)	C **8 NUMBERS** (e.g. 12.12.1972)
Major Period	9 years	9 years	9 years
Sub-Period	1 year, 6 months	1 year, 3 months, 13 days	1 year, 1 month, 15 days
Minor Period	3 months	2 months, 6 days	1 month, 2 days

\# For the 9-year period from 54 to 63 years, the number 4 will again have influence.

Thus, in the above manner, numbers from the date of birth will repeat in a regular cycle.

SUB-PERIODS AND MINOR PERIODS

Now, the above major period of 9 years is too broad a division to arrive at meaningful predictions. Hence, these 9-year periods are further sub-divided into **Sub-Periods.** These sub-periods are then further reduced to periods of a few months called **Minor Periods**.

Based on the number of digits in the date of birth, i.e. 6 numbers, 7 numbers or 8 numbers, **we have three categories of sub-periods and minor periods**, as given in the periodicity table below:

In the above calculations for category A, the division results in no remainder. Whereas in categories B and C, small remainders occur but are not considered as they amount to a few hours for each sub-division.

```
To find out age as on        5.5.2000
Subtract date of birth       2.2.1972
                             ----------
                             3.3.  28
```

0 to 9	9 to 18	18 to 27	27 to 36	36 to 45	45 to 54	54 to 63	63 to 72
2	2	1	9	7	2	2	2

The detailed calculations for all ages and categories are given later for reference in Chapter 27. All one has to do is refer to the index and relevant column/s.

Let's look at examples of the working models for all these categories.

CATEGORY A: 6 NUMBERS

Date of Birth: 2.2.1972

This person's age on the date of calculation is 28 years, 3 months and 3 days.

Now we have to allot the major period, sub-period and minor period numbers.

Major Period: 9 years

As mentioned earlier, numbers are allotted from the date of birth in a continuous sequence, starting from the first digit — in this case, it is 2. As the date of birth has only 6 numbers, at 54 to 63 years, we have the first digit of the date of birth repeating. Here, the number 9 is highlighted since this person's age is between 27 to 36 years and it will be his major period number.

Sub-Period: 1 year, 6 months

Since the date of birth is of 6 numbers, these numbers only will be re-allotted for the sub-period too. Now, for the above date of birth, the actual

27 to 28½	28½ to 30	30 to 31½	31½ to 33	33 to 34½	34½ to 36
9	7	2	2	2	1

27 to 27-3	27-3 to 27-6	27-6 to 27-9	27-9 to 28
9	7	2	2
28 to 28-3	28-3 to 28-6		
2	1		

age is 28 years, 3 months and 3 days, falling in the major period of 27 to 36 years. So, for this period, the sub-period (of 1½ years duration) will be When allotting numbers for the sub-periods, we **start with the number of the major period under which the person's current actual age comes**, which in the above case is 9. The rest of the numbers are then allotted in a continuous sequence from the date of birth. Here, 9 is highlighted because this person's age is in the first sub-period group.

Minor Period: 3 months

For the above date of birth, the actual age is 28 years, 3 months and 3 days — which, in the sub-period, falls in the first group of 27 to 28½ years. When we reduce this to a minor period (of 3 months duration), we get Here again, to allot numbers, we **start with the number of the sub-period of the actual age**, which in the above case is 9. The rest of the numbers will be allotted in sequence from the sub-period.

Hence, for the date of birth 2.2.1972, the age as on 5.5.2000 is 28 years, 3 months and 3 days. So, the major period number is 9, the sub-period number is 9, and the minor period number is 1. For all the periods, marking the numbers below them makes sequential allocation easy.

CATEGORY B: 7 NUMBERS

To find out age as on	5. 5.2000
Subtract date of birth	2.12.1972
Actual age	3. 5. 27

0 to 9	9 to 18	18 to 27	27 to 36	36 to 45	45 to 54	54 to 63	63 to 72
2	1	2	1	9	7	2	2

27 to 28-3-13	28-3-13 to 29-6-26	29-6-26 to 30-10-9
1	9	7
30-10-9 to 32-1-22	32-1-22 to 33-5-5	33-5-5 to 34-8-18
2	2	1
34-8-18 to 36-0-0		
2		

27-0-0 to 27-2-6	27-2-6 to 27-4-12	27-4-12 to 27-6-18
1	9	7
27-6-18 to 27-8-24	27-8-24 to 17-11-0	27-11-0 to 28-1-6
2	2	1
28-1-6 to 28-3-12		
2		

Date of Birth: 2.12.1972

Major Period: 9 years

Sub-Period: 1 year, 3 months, 13 days

Minor Period: 0 years, 2 months, 6 days

CATEGORY C: 8 NUMBERS

Date of Birth: 10.12.1955

```
To find out age as on        5.  5. 2000
Subtract date of birth      10. 12.1955
                            --------------
Actual age                  25.  4.  44
```

0 to 9	9 to 18	18 to 27	27 to 36	36 to 45	45 to 54	54 to 63	63 to 72
1	0	1	2	1	9	5	5

36 to 37-1-15	37-1-15 to 38-3	38-3 to 39-4-15	39-4-15 to 40-6
1	9	5	5
40-6 to 41-7-15	41-7-15 to 42-9	42-9 to 43-10-15	43-10-15 to 45
1	0	1	2

43-1-15 to 44-0-6	44-0-6 to 44-1-27	44-1-27 to 44-3-18
2	1	9
44-3-18 to 44-5-9	44-5-9 to 44-7-0	44-7-0 to 44-8-21
5	5	1
44-8-21 to 44-10-12	44-10-12 to 45	
0	1	

Major Period: 9 years

Sub-Period: 1 year, 1 month, 15 days

Minor Period: 0 years, 1 month, 21 days

For easy application, remember these salient points about the different periods and allocation of numbers:

Major Period Numbers

The allotted numbers in the major period show the **fluctuations in life for 9 years**. It can be likened to leaving the house for a journey where the destination will be reached at the end of the ninth year.

Sub-Period Numbers

The allotted numbers in the sub-period **reveal the yearly progress** of the journey of 9 years.

Minor Period Numbers

The allotted numbers here **reveal the monthly progress for every year** of the journey of 9 years.

For all the periods, the marriage date and every individual's date of birth affect the fluctuations either favourably or adversely.

Once we have done the allocation of numbers, we can predict on the basis of details given later in the chapters on the interpretation and effects of allotted numbers.

Chapter 8: If You Born On The 3. (Third) Or 12th (Twelfth), Or 21st (Twenty First) Or 30th (Thirtieth) Of Any Month Than Kindly Read The Following:

BIRTH NUMBER THREE

Happy outgoing, forever, optimistic, vivacious, talkative, scattered all these describe the threes. Lovers of social life and recreation, Threes do not enjoy hard physical employment. They may excel at sales and will always have several projects going on at once. Work must feel creative for them to be happy. They are not overly concern about money or the future.

They are spontaneous and impulsive. They must learn to be focused and not overly self-indulge. When positive they bring joy and light to all situations. All Threes easily overcome physical illness. They are charming quick to see the humor in any situation but can be somewhat unreliable. They may spread themselves over several projects because they like to keep themselves busy.

They are energetic, but easily distracted. Their social life is of a great concern to them. Having many friends they need to budget a sizeable amount of gifts because they are also generous.

They love spontaneous get-together and may be the one in the office to suggest the going out of drinks or taking up a collection for a birthday party. They naturally embellish stories and events.

You are known for youthfulness, certain intensity in style and while friends may laugh about your scattered ness, you are love by them.

As we are aware that numbers have their own unique qualities and personalities and each of them having different signs. To know a good understanding of how numbers influence and affect us, we ought to get to gather and know each single-digit number in detail as how a person carries his own, personality his weakness and his strength of will power.

Detail description of the unique combination and union between the numbers 1 and 2 has been penned above as the main numbers of the main number family while describing the deep contradiction in nature of each of the number and their personalities.

Now, we move on to what could be considered the result of their union: The number 3, an extraordinarily talented child. They are like a small gifted kids who are still under the protection of its elders somewhat spoiled, and always in need of guidance. However, the most of the number 3 are in the field of creation.

The powerful feelings, ideas and visions of the imagination, person with number 3s will seek a career in art. Their social skills are also excellent.

Many are drawn to three in their charts and are even willing to forgive traits like a lack of focus and direction, a habit of coping others. Also a caliber to finish projects and an not willing to take responsibility.

It is easy for number three to enjoy day-to-day life as long as everything is well, but when challenges arise it becomes quite evident, that most of the three's focus has been on that exterior, leaving its fortitude at bay.

Number three succumbs to difficulties unless friends and family move in to support it. Having birth date as 3 is likely to add a good of vitality to your life. The energy of 3 allows you to bounce back rapidly from all kinds of setbacks, be it mental or physical.

They have a natural ability to express themselves in public, and always make a very good impression. Good with words, they excel in writing, speaking, and possibly singing. They are energetic and always a good conversationalist. They are affectionate and loving, but sometimes too sensitive.

IF YOU WERE BORN ON THE 12th

You have one of the most magnetic birth dates. You have an exceptional ability to express yourself, be convincing, and persuade others. Your mind goes right to the heart at any issue. You are idealistic, yet logical and can be brilliant.

You are easily bored and often tired of people ones you have picked their brains. You have a great need to charm and need to flirt. Your eye for color and design, especially in photography, is outstanding. You love the media-movies,

Magazines, television and keep up to date on who is whom. You are something of a celebrity of yourself. The number 12 is a complete cycle of experience and when an individual has number 12 as the birth number it leans towards a higher consciousness.

This number points to a group of developed souls who have accumulated an unusual inner strength. Their old habits need to be changed. The soul then attracts what it needs as a learning experience.

Number 12 should tend to be alert to every situation, to be suspicious of those who offer a false flattery and those who use it to gain their own ends.

Number 12 represents the learning process of all levels, and the sacrifice necessary to achieve the wisdom on both Spiritual and Intellectual levels. The number 12 generally need a partner who is honesty in their communication. They are quick to get attracted to people who are bright, happy, independent and lively.

Laughter is quite an important part of their lives and they have inquiring minds to collect data on interesting subjects because they enjoy mental stimulation and enjoyment of mental nature. People get attracted towards them as they possess a wide range of knowledge about the world and its people. They don't like being told that they cannot do a thing. The more talented they become, about their abilities they become more cautious about it. They possess a high degree of artistic talent that emerges in virtually everything. They take seriously, their home, cooking, the way they express themselves, when committed to.

They enjoy more entertaining people with stories, jokes, or witty remarks. They have plenty of vitality and are especially talented in the verbal and writing skills. The positive aspects: imaginative and quick-witted versatile, energetic and professional, perceptive attributes and abilities family consciousness, friendly in their relationships, and rather shy.

IF YOU WERE BORN ON THE 21st

You may be a bit quieter and less impulsive then other Threes, very sensitive and more likely to think things through before speaking. You have a great imagination and may be prone to dreaming, perhaps writing poetry. You may be natural singer or songwriter. You may be content to have fewer, but closer friends then other Threes.

You are high strung and should avoid analyzing things too much.

You may find you have a tendency of infatuations (due to seeing people in a rosier light through your imagination and sense of drama). You may be gullible. You love pleasure and aesthetic pursuits. You definitely avoid manual labor if at all possible.

You would have the energy to bounce back rapidly from early setbacks, of physical or mental nature. At times there would restlessness in your nature, but you seem to be able to show an easygoing attitude and nature in you, You have a special and natural ability to express yourself in public, and you always make a very good impression on others. You dream of artistic expression; writing, painting, music. You would seek to more freely express your inner feeling and obtain more enjoyment from life. You also dream of being more popular, likable, and appreciated .Good in literary pursuits, you excel well in singing writing, and speaking, you are energetic and always are good conversation.

You have a good and keen imagining power, and are talented in writing and verbal skills. But it is often seen that you generally tend to waste your energies and become involved with too many things which are unnatural and superficial.

Your mind is quite practical emanation and rational despite having this tendency and you are able to jump out of the awkward situations. You are quite affectionate charming and loving, but at the same time very sensitive. You are subject to rapid ups and downs in your life and you often take it as a very serious matter. You are highly creative, a vivacious soul and dynamic a creature who carries immense vigor & energy and believes in living every moment of life.

You are generally possessed with a strong will to succeed. You have a social gift. Your imagination is highly charged.

You get along well with others and generally enjoy people's company and their environment condition. You are quick witted and can think on your feet. Both your mind and body are vital and seemingly sparklingly with life.

You are talented in verbal skills, scribbling, writing and speaking. You can be a successful, writer, editor cum artist. You are energetic inspiring and enthusiastic and willing to learn whatever comes in your way. You can uplift or enlighten a party or social gatherings and may serve as the life of the party. You feel pleasure in becoming a limelight of your social gatherings. You are an excellent speaker and salesman. Your focus your energies deeply in a specific field make the most of your life as winner.

Your imagination runs out of control. You must develop yourself and your talents in order to make the most of your life. You can easily let charm and wit pass for outstanding work. Your challenge is to ground and focus your energies deeply in a specific field or subject. Your love runs deep and you can be passionate. More often you seem to be on the receiving end of affection, simply because people are charmed by you or attracted to your charismatic and dynamic personality.

People with 21 as their number are the ones who would party hard after working hard as they are sincere personalities but never forget to live life. The people with this number carry a great charisma in their presence and are magnetic other people generally like to be with them.

Positive qualities: creative, a vivacious writer, editor cum artist. Charismatic and dynamic personality inspiration, creativity, love unions, long lasting relationships and verbal skills

Negative traits: imagination runs out of control disappointment, fear of change dependency, nervousness, over emotionalism, lack of vision, and unnecessary involvement in too many things.

IF YOU WERE BORN ON THE 30th

You have exceptional high energy. Your enthusiasm is infectious; you can motivate and persuade others. You are outspoken and have a flair for having just the right word or fact to win a argument. You may have strong psychic ability. You would be a excellent teacher, actor, or musician. You would make a wonderful minister. You are serious and intense about what interest you, but will find it difficult to fulfill old promises. Like other Threes, you are flirtatious. Guard against a tendency to drink too much or overspend on cloths and socializing.

Chapter 9: How To Work Out Your Numerology Numbers

With the benefits of numerology still fresh in your mind, you're probably anxious to start working out your own numerology numbers. Below are several of the different numbers you can use to get guidance in your life, plus the way to determine this number for yourself. You can use these numbers to find out more about yourself, the people around you, and your future.

Name Number

To discover your name number, you need to take the numbers that represent each number in your name and add them together until they make a single digit. The Name Number, sometimes called the Name Ruling Number, is one of the most frequently used numbers in numerology, so learning yours will help you in many ways.

Here are the letters and the numbers they represent

A, J, S = 1

B, K, T = 2

C, L, U = 3

D, M, V = 4

E, N, W = 5

F, O, X = 6

G, P, Y = 7

H, Q, Z = 8

I, R = 9

Motivation Number

If you want to know why you behave the way you do and why you make the decisions you do, one way to find out is by finding your Motivation Number. The more you understand about what motivates you, the more you'll be able to control your actions and reactions. For more information on this side of yourself, you should also consider looking into your Karmic Name Number.

To find your Motivation Number, you should take the vowels from your name and add them together until all you have is a single digit number

A = 1

U = 3

E = 5

O = 6

Y = 7

I = 9

Karmic Name Number

The next number you can learn is your karmic number. This number gives you an idea of where your karmic scales are currently. By knowing how your scales are balanced, you'll know if you need to send more good into the world to improve your current karma. The Karmic Name Number can also reveal to you what emotions you have, deep inside. When you know what your true wishes, fears, concerns, and hopes are, you'll be better able to understand why you act the way you do, even if it is subconsciously.

To get your Karmic Name Number, you'll need to add together all the consonants of your first official name. Don't use vowels and don't use nicknames or chosen names. You have to use the name you were given at birth for this to work. Once you've added all the consonants from your first name together, you should keep adding them until you get a single digit number. This is your Karmic Name Number.

J, S = 1

B, K, T = 2

C, L = 3

D, M, V = 4

N, W = 5

F, X = 6

G, P, Y = 7

H, Q, Z = 8

R = 9

Day Number

Moving away from letter numerology, your Day Number is one of the most important numerology numbers you need to know. Day Numbers will show you the major influencers in your life and bring clarity to the reasons you react and interact the way you do. Also, the Day Number can help you see what type of life you should be leading to reach your success.

To discover your Day Number, add all the number from your birth day together. So, for example, if you were born on June 12, you would add 1 + 2 = 3. Three would be your Day Number.

Destiny Number

Finally, you can also learn your Destiny Number. This is the number that will inform you about what you need to do to interact properly with everything around you and what actions you should take to reach success. It shows you the ways success will be presented to you, so when it arrives, you'll be better able to realize it and take the path that leads you to where you want to go.

To find your Destiny Number, you need to add all the numbers of your birthdate together. Using the same date above as an example, if you were born on June 12, 1983, you would add together the following numbers:

6 (June) + 1 + 2 (12th) + 1 + 9 + 8 + 3 (1983) = 30.

3 + 0 = 3

So, if your birthday was June 12, 1983, your Destiny Number would be 3.

By knowing all your numerology numbers, studying their meanings, and listening to their instructions, you can get a better idea of how to live your life. You can slowly change your lifestyle and the way you react to your surroundings to live better.

Chapter 10: The Destiny Number

Now your name is hardly the only way to work out a number for yourself, there is also the numbers of your birth date. You simply need to take each digit of your birth date and then add them up until you have a total and then add them again until you have a single digit unless your birth date adds up to eleven or twenty-two. While your name number will tell you a great deal about who you are, the number you get from your birth date, which is known as your destiny number, will tell you about what course in life would be best for you to take.

Destiny Number One – If your destiny number is one then you are born to lead. You could be drawn to politics or professional sport as these will be areas where your ambition can be given full rein. Also, the area of business will be good for you with the chances of promotion being high. You are decisive and in control but the danger is that you will be unsympathetic and that can lead to you making enemies. Be careful not to tread on too many toes.

Destiny Number Two – If your destiny number is two then you will probably be drawn to careers where you can exercise your sympathetic skills; nursing would be a good choice for you. Counselling is another good option as you are an exceptionally good listener. The danger for you is that in your hurry to help others, you forget about your own needs and if you ignore your own needs for too long it can breed resentment. Don't be afraid to stand up for yourself and it's not selfish to think of your own needs occasionally.

Destiny Number Three – If your destiny number is three then ideally you would be best in a job connected to the travel industry. Writing travel books or exploring or even being a tour guide would work well for you. There is also scope for travelling in a spiritual or mental way; you could enjoy studying, particularly philosophy or religion. You could be a good writer or teacher but the danger will always be that your hatred of restrictions will cause you to flout the rules in a dangerous way. You need to find a career that suits your need for freedom and independence.

Destiny Number Four – If your destiny number is four then you will work best in large corporations or organisations where your superb attention to detail will be noticed. You like to be in environments you can control so an office is probably best for you. You do not like to be spontaneous, you like everything to be planned out and the danger is that your love of the rules can give you tunnel vision so that you forget everything else.

But you are such a hard worker and so efficient that you are bound to be promoted. Also, your incredible grasp of facts and figures will impress anyone who is your boss. And your tireless efforts are ability to work almost unlimited overtime will help but just don't let your boss use you as a doormat.

Destiny Number Five – When your destiny number is five then it is obvious that you will be brilliant at communicating. Any job that allows you to share this skill will be great for you. You would be a great DJ or TV presenter; also you could be a writer or a journalist. You're likely to have a very quick grasp of situations, able to think on your feet and act accordingly. Your knowledge probably won't be in-depth but you can employ researchers to help you fill in the gaps.

The danger for you is that you love new things and ideas so much that you tend to start things all the time but not follow through leaving a mountain of unfinished tasks which if left unattended too long can become just too high to scale. Either learn to discipline yourself to finish things or get someone to help you with that.

But you are brilliant at brainstorming and your verbal dexterity could see you do well in advertising where your inspired jingles could sell sand to the Arabs! You love gadgets and will be quick at getting to grips with them; mastering the latest technology is never a problem for someone like you.

Destiny Number Six – If you're destiny number is six then you are one of the beautiful people. You are inspired by beautiful things and are not happy in an ugly or disruptive environment. You would excel as an interior designer or anything where you can use your skill at creating beautiful places. You are probably interested in crafting and making lovely things, such as clothes and jewellery. You have an excellent eye for colour and design so a career in fashion is a possibility as well.

Your weakness is that because you hate chaos and unpleasantness so much when scenes erupt, you tend to cut and run away rather than stand your ground and unscrupulous people could use that against you, creating scenes just to make you back down. But your intense dislike of scenes means that as a rule you tend to behave very well to people, being pleasant and kind and very good mannered so the chances are you will be very well liked.

Destiny Number Seven – People with the destiny number of seven often have strong links to religion of one sort or another. You will have a mystical sense of longing in your soul that will make you want to explore spiritual values. It's not unknown for sevens to become religious leaders or gurus of some sort. You will probably have a fascination with meditation and the religious beliefs can sometimes be quite unorthodox. You will have a dreamy side to your nature as if you are listening to some celestial music that no-one but you can hear.

The danger for you is that with your obsession with the spiritual you can neglect practical matters and end up with a pile of unpaid bills on your doormat simply because you have neglected to keep up with the day to day payments that life demands. Try to make sure that you keep at least one foot on the ground because dealing with the practical things quickly will save you having to sort out a big mess that will only drag you away from your soul searching for longer.

Destiny Number Eight – If your destiny number is eight then it is possible that you view life as a battleground and you must win at all costs. You will be extremely competitive and you could do well in professional sport. The armed forces is another area where you might excel. You physical strength and stamina will be excellent and you do not tire easily. The danger is that your aggression can get you into trouble. You need to find a way to focus your aggression so that it becomes a positive thing.

You have a go-getting style which can see you achieve a lot and it is not difficult for you to outperform rivals but despite your advantages you cannot win all the time and you must learn to be magnanimous in defeat.

Destiny Number Nine — If your destiny number is nine then you are likely to be quite serious and deep. You will struggle to be light hearted and have fun. You have a tendency to test things to extreme limits and so need to avoid excessive drink and alcohol because it can be difficult for you to know when to stop. You tend to go at things with an all or nothing attitude. Your lesson in life is to learn balance.

Your ability to almost regenerate and re-invent your self means you can do many different things but unlike fives who will tend to do many things all at once you will throw yourself totally into something, only to reject it later and throw yourself into something completely different. Your current project will tend to be all-consuming for you and it's possible that you will forgo sleep and food to get it done.

Destiny Number Eleven — If your destiny number is eleven then you were born to teach. It's quite possible that you could become a teacher but there are more way to teach than just teaching in schools. You could be involved in training or you could just teach people by letting them watch you lead your life. You can lead by example but you must remember that people can also learn from you being a bad example. You have the potential to be a great force for evil or good depending on your ethics.

The best that you can be is a shining beacon of light and goodness; the worst that you can be is very bad indeed and you can be sure there will be lots of people who would learn to behave better from your potential bad example but that may not be how you would want to be remembered.

Destiny Number Twenty Two – If your destiny number is twenty two then you have the potential to either be a creator or a destroyer. In whatever field you choose to go into you can either make magnificent progress and constantly break new ground taking your chosen filed into new and better way all the time or you can create chaos and destroy everything around you including yourself. It is up to you to harness your enormous potential in the best ways possible.

There is a sense that in destroying things you can create anew but this may not be the most productive way of doing things although some tearing down of old outdated systems can be necessary and useful. It will be important for you to try to harness your powers in positive ways and bring out the best in yourself and other people.

Chapter 11: Calculating Your Life Path

There has long been a belief that we are born knowing all that is needed to guide us through life however, we must understand ourselves, learn to trust our instinct and fully comprehend and make sense of the experiences of life before our inner knowledge falls into place.

So, there will be much to learn and consider. Some of the lessons of life are easy while others may take longer. This is where the life path number is important. It is often referred to as the Birth Force Number or you may hear the term Lesson Number, but it equates to the route you should follow throughout your life so to achieve the most success. By understanding and of course, using the life path number, this will save you time and energy as you progress in life.

The life path number is derived by using your birthdate and so, this is a consistent number right throughout your life. To calculate the life path number, you need the day, month and 4-digit year of your birth. You have to know the numerical value for each month before you begin.

Month to number table

- January1
- February2.
- March3
- Apri4
- May5
- June6
- July7
- August8.
- September9.
- October1
- November2.
- December 3.

If the month of your birthday is a double-digit number, you must reduce it to a single digit as in the table above.

Write down the month, day and four-digit year of your birthdate. To make it easier, write the numbers associated with them above the date, and then add the reduced values so that you have single digits.

Here's an example: 5 + 9 +1+9+6+5 **May 9, 1965.** Add these single digits 5 + 9 +1+9+6+5 = 35 and then, add 3+5 to get 8 It is that simple.

Life path number 1

If this is your life path, you need to start believing in yourself and to value yourself fully. You have all the abilities for life, but you must trust in yourself. You are important, even if others do not always agree with the things you say or do. You are fully able to stand up for yourself and to express your views and you do not need to find approval from others. At times, it may feel as if others possess or control you, so you must learn to take control of situations around you. Endeavour to be more decisive.

Increase your ability to embrace courage and resist the temptation to give into others. If you strongly believe you're right, stick to your beliefs. Do not lose your temper – you may be prone to do this if stressed. If your life path number is 19 (before it was reduced) be especially aware of how you respond to stress.

Be creative and endeavor to stamp your creativity on life. You have excellent research skills and your ideal job could be in a research position or developing software or working at a university. Your leadership skills may need a little work so to initiate projects with confidence and you should believe in your ability to develop new ideas. Work on increasing mental agility, develop strong business acumen and learn to think quickly and respond to any issues.

Life path number 2

If this is your life path number, it's time to improve your powers of persuasion. Try to be a little more diplomatic and tactful in life and take time to research all the facts before deciding. It's important to develop a greater ability to compromise where possible and if need be, take on the role of mediator and negotiator and you will be able to help others resolve any difficult situations so that there is an amicable solution.

Work on self-assertion so that you can be sure others will not take advantage of you as this happens sometimes. Equally, you can be a little too sensitive at times and may take everything personally. So, it is important to learn from constructive criticism rather than taking it to heart. Try to be more flexible in life and to go with the flow, rather than being overwhelmed by difficulties. Sometimes, you fail to reach out for help, but it is important that you do so.

You may find that your ideal career is one where you work with the public, equipment or even machinery. You excel at work that involves studying the minutest details, so perhaps researching, medicine, analytical work or even, choosing religion as a career. Continue to keep learning and be willing to share your knowledge and work of others.

Life path number 3

If this is your life path number, confidence is an issue. As such, it's important to continue to develop your self-confidence levels and to give them a boost. You're prone to shyness, but by working on your social skills , this will help you to feel better in social situations generally. To increase communication, it can be useful to learn more vocabulary, and this helps you to express yourself. Remember to have fun in life but aim to be more optimistic rather than focusing on negative aspects. Focus on the more charming aspects of yourself of which there are many. You may be prone to being critical of others but try to avoid doing this. Your ideal career may be one where success comes from entertainment, literary or artistic pursuits and it can be useful to find creative outlets for your talents. Focus just on one thing at a time and learn each thing well as this increase's confidence and self-esteem.

Life path number 4

If this is your life path number, it's important to accept responsibility for your own life. Try to appreciate the value of things that you have already rather than just in financial terms. Buy only what is needed and not just about what you want to have. Consider what is needed as you may find that you spend too much. To gain success, you need to acquire as much knowledge as is possible and be prepared to work towards your goals.

Develop practical systems so to make life more efficient. You may find that your ideal career is in project management, event planning or, film production, in fact, anything where you have rules and regulations to follow.

Life path number 5

If your life path number is 5, it's time to embrace change. Learn to be more flexible, but also, don't be afraid to take some risks now and then. Develop a greater interest in current events and be more open-minded in thinking and relish being more adaptive to difficult situations. When it comes to romance, listen to your intuition.

Focus fully on your commitments, but do not multi-task, but focus on one thing at a time. Sometimes, you miss out on opportunities and so, make sure to assess and reach out for opportunities if they sound appealing. Do not hold back. You may find your ideal career is in marketing, sales, entertainment and advertising, but in your career, you must continue to progress forward as this will keep you engaged.

Life path number 6

If this is your life path number, it's time to be more responsible especially around the house and to attend to outstanding chores. Take responsibility and do not shy away from it. On an emotional sense, allow yourself to feel and to give love. You may find this difficult but persevere. You have your own way of dealing with things in life but understand that not everyone acts or thinks in the same way.

Be a little more flexible and avoid being overly stubborn. Expand your horizons but do so within the community through volunteering or perhaps, helping others by giving advice. Your ideal career may be in counselling, interior design, catering or working with animals or children.

Life path number 7

With this life path number, it is important to investigate the metaphysical mysteries of life as you are drawn towards them and this will help you feel satisfied. Always strive to seek more information and do not be afraid to ask questions rather than taking things at face value. As you learn more, share this knowledge with others too. It's important to embrace being alone at times without feeling emotionally lonely and sometimes, you struggle with this. It can help you to discover nature around you or to simply to enjoy some quiet evenings at home so that you can rest. Good communication will be important to you so develop your vocabulary and your ability to write and speak. Your ideal career may be in analytical studies or research, metaphysics, psychic studies, investigative reporting, detective work, nutrition, engineering or computers.

Life path number 8

If you have life path number 8, try to create more balance and well-being in life. This includes diet, exercise and health. You should also take control of your financial well-being. It's important to develop the ability to handle power, money and the success that comes with it. Sometimes, you struggle with this but not through a lack of ability, perhaps, a lack of self-belief at times.

Learn to delegate responsibilities to others as you cannot do everything yourself. Don't rush through tasks, take the time to complete them properly. Do not place self-limitations upon you but instead, relish the idea of finding success on a great scale. You may find your ideal career is in coaching, organizing, supervising or working in sports, real estate or even, property management.

Life path number 9

If you have this life path number, you may wish to work in a humanitarian area. It is important for you to show compassion to others and to inspire them in life. Try to develop an interest in world affairs and take time to explore your love of the arts. Your ideal career path maybe where you are helping others, such as medicine – nursing or as a doctor. But, you may consider being a therapist, a teacher, working in the arts – including television or films but especially if travel is involved. Focus on your ideas for money-making but let others handle the details.

Master life path number 11

If you have a Master life path of 11, it is often believed that you arrived here on Earth with very few lessons to learn. Even so, much will be required as you travel through life. You feel at your happiest when you are helping others to share your energy, your philosophies in life, idealism, but learn to accept others, just as they are. It is important to embrace gratitude.

Master life path number 22

Prepared to broaden your horizons, expand your thinking and let that inner you shine. Develop international connections but embrace contentment through planning and organizing for the benefits of others.

Chapter 12: Caretaker And Giver; The Public Relations Expert

The Moon presides over this Birthday, and is indicative of strong water or air aspects in an astrological chart, such as Cancer, Libra, Scorpio, Gemini, Pisces or Aquarius, and can weaken the power of a fire (Aries, Leo, Sagittarius) or earth (Taurus, Virgo, Capricorn) sign and lessen the effect of any stronger Façade number. The cycles of the moon strongly influence the emotional flux of the 2 Birthday. In personal readings, I always tell 2 Birthday women to check their emotions against their menstrual flow cycle, especially if the flow occurs during a Full Moon. The 2 Birthday's ongoing challenge is to avoid getting hysterical or irrational when their royal self-image is dented. Its presence in a Birthday number or cycle adds pensiveness, gentleness, flexibility, indecisiveness, and a sense of beauty. His architectural models showed that even

Adolph Hitler, my prime 2 example, had an innate sense of beauty. Flexibility is the positive catch word for the 2. A 2 will rationalize its indecisiveness as merely looking at both sides of an issue, but a 2 Birthday sees as many facets to any situation as there are on a diamond. This indecisiveness nature is most pronounced in someone born on the 11th. Innate moodiness sometimes causes the 2 Birthday to show lack of consideration that it would not tolerate in others. It expects forgiveness, but it doesn't forgive easily.

One problem 2s have is that of wasting time. Whereas, 1 is the number of initiation and 3 that of change, 2 carries with it the tendency to hang in between, to vacillate, and remain in limbo. It's a great negotiating number, but significant change is not possible with the 2. It's much more difficult to achieve and takes a much more conscientious effort. The first example that comes to mind are two of the worst riots in Los Angeles history. Both started on 2 Days, but neither accomplished anything in themselves. Some of the best negotiated treaties have occurred on 2 Days.

This is the Birthday of the giver, caretaker, nurturer and king or queen of denial. This is the Birthday number of the eternally youthful looking. One memorable example is from a party where I gave readings some years ago. I met a woman who appeared to be about 60 years old. She turned out to be 85 and a 2 Birthday. 2 is a feminine number. This helps 2 men understand women and, at times, manipulate them. 2s need lots of approval and love, and they need to be needed. This is their weakness, and they need to be careful not to let themselves be manipulated by either sex for the sake of approval. At times they value approval more than honesty. 2s many times choose friends who will tell them what they want to hear instead of the truth. 2s might even follow a crowd for the sake of approval. A 2 criminal most likely is playing "follow the leader" or is trying to win peer approval.

He may delude himself into thinking that he is leading the pack, but the pack is leading him. This need for love and approval sometimes couples with their giving, nurturing side to their undoing because it causes them to do things for those who don't reciprocate. 2s can compensate for the overly giving weakness by bringing out their innate stubbornness when someone tries to use them. Flexibility is the positive catchword for the 2. 2s are inherently indecisive. Instead of seeing two sides of an issue, they see and weigh out too many options, which slows down making life-changing decisions and is a way to put off the future. Some strong Pinnacles can remedy this indecisiveness. The 2's ability to attract all sorts of people inevitably leads them to the right people and the right place at the right time, as well as the worst people at the worst time.

2s can be excellent liars because their denial side helps them feel as though they are telling the truth at the moment they are lying. 2s know how to add gloss to anything or anyone. They are great at making themselves and others look favorable. For these reasons, 2s are natural public relations people. They excel in public relations, sales, customer relations, negotiators, mediators or any other type of work in which they soothe the savage beast in others. Many become nurses and therapists of various sorts. They also make great teachers. 2s are among the greatest of visionaries and can bring on the greatest of fanfares, as shown by the 2 Birthday Surrealist artist, Salvador Dali. They often fancy themselves to be queens or kings, but the strength of their regality is wholly dependent on the strength of their Pinnacles, not taking forever to decide on a course of action and their willingness to face the issues. My favorite example is Marie Antoinette. She was the Queen of France at the outset of the French Revolution. When she was told that the French masses were starving, her only reply was "Let them eat cake." I wonder if that statement came to mind when she was laid down for her beheading. This is a warning of sorts to all 2s. Face the problems before the blade comes down. The most important emotional challenge for any 2 Birthday is to separate friends from those who use him and, like his 6 Birthday cousin, not to let the users guilt trip him into giving in to everyone else's needs and wants at the sacrifice of his life and sanity. 2s make the biggest difference in the lives of their loved ones and those they wish to help when they learn not to try so hard to make things better for everyone. The key idea is to find real friends, not just people who are cheering the loudest with approval. 2 Birthdays are the best of support personnel, but they need to think long and hard before taking on the stressful responsibility of leadership unless Pinnacle numbers support this. "Love me" is their motto. Men with a 2 Birthday are lovers, not fighters, though they often go to great lengths to hide or disprove this, especially if one or more Pinnacles set them up to be the proverbial tough guys. 2s are extremely hard and devoted workers, especially when they receive the right amount of praise, though they need to be on guard about taking on more than they can handle.

The 2 needs to be wary of denying unresolved emotional issues that cause him to be led by the crowd just for approval. They should beware of spending money to win love and approval, yet they can compensate for this weakness by bringing out their innate stubbornness when they are pushed against the proverbial wall. Adolf Hitler, born on the 20th, merely was compensating for inner insecurities by acting in a bold fashion, but any real resistance from the German people or world leaders would have made him back down very quickly. The 2 Birthday usually has a weak physical nature unless there are strong numbers in the numerological chart and beneficial aspects in the astrological chart. An overabundance of 2s in a numerological chart would increase this tendency toward a weak body or a weak disposition in dealing with others and it would hinder the individuals earning ability. Many 2s compensate for the money problem with the innate ability to make a dollar bill squeak, especially when protecting the family. Its perpetual luck that pulls them out of a jam when needed and the ability to attract people who can support or help them out. The latter being part of the 2's public relations skills.

Groucho Marx, born on the 2nd, showed all of these traits during the stock market crash of 1929 when he lost a quarter of a million dollars but was able to make ends meet by continually drumming up work and belt tightening. He was aided by his 8 Facade which gave him an air of authority in business dealings. Adolf Hitler was infamous among his military leaders for refusing to heed their views on strategy. Maintaining this attitude for too long eventually wreaked havoc on his nervous system. This is probably why Hitler needed large doses of medication as his tactics became the cause of Germany's increased battlefield losses.

The statement of the Polish writer, Joseph Conrad, "We live as we dream: alone," is the trademark characteristic of the 2 Birthdate. Moodiness and, at times, a withdrawn nature that verges on secretiveness, which, despite the 2's need for approval, can cause the 2 to be a loner that few of his associates and friends truly know, a self-imposed emotional exile, especially when things don't work out for the 2. The 2 Birthday greatly aided Adolf Hitler and Joseph Stalin in maintaining their secretiveness. 2s are nostalgic. They often hold onto memories and paraphernalia long after either the memory of the item holds any real meaning for them. This makes denial too easy for the 2 Birthday. For all the evil that he ordered upon Europe, I seriously doubt that Hitler would have had the nerve to carry out any of the actions of his henchmen because of the 2's soft nature. After all, he saw very little of the actual brutality he ordered and there is no proof that he ever visited the concentration camps.

The same rule applies to Joseph Stalin. Though he was known among Russians as "The Butcher" because he ordered the execution of millions of his compatriots who opposed him, there is no record that he killed anyone himself. He merely stayed in the Kremlin and signed stacks of death orders for those who were said to have opposed him. Trying to pull them out of their shells causes further clamming up or an emotional outburst. Tantrums are a favorite means to an end for 2s. Hitler threw tantrums as apocalyptic as the destruction he brought upon Europe and North Africa. 2s naturally draw all sorts of people, so they need to be careful what they wish for. Hitler was known for his hypnotic-like charisma in front of the people. A 2 has a natural intrinsic ability to charm the masses, which is why they will do well in public relations.

Because of the strong feminine aspect of the number 2, the women tend to be Earth Mothers, and the men tend to be more gentle or indecisive than you would expect from males. Mahatma Gandhi is one of the most prominent examples of the 2's male gentleness. A 2 woman needs a man, even when she has withdrawn into her shell. She need not worry about being able to attract one for she can expect to remain feminine all her life, even if she lives to the age of Solomon.

A 2 Birthday wants to be the boss, but being the boss might be too much of a toll on the 2's nerves. They can present themselves or someone else in the best possible way, and since their financial fortunes always come easily while working for others, they do well in public relations, or as negotiators and mediators. Hitler was a top-notch public relations man to have convinced enough voters to elect him Chancellor of Germany. So, too, with Joseph Stalin, as his ability to put his best self forward at the Allied conferences gave him the nickname, "Uncle Joe."

A 2 secretary always is the epitome of the executive assistant, being the best clerical back up and the best front person for a company. Directly supervising large or unruly groups is too trying for the 2 Birthday, so, as a leader, the 2 easily could feel pushed into a corner when faced with lack of cooperation or defiance. As teachers, 2s work best with older children or adults.

2s are extremely hard and devoted workers when they are devoted to their employers and enjoy their work, especially when they are given the sufficient amount of praise. Hitler was known to spend hours studying military strategy and weaponry as well as ways to improve the daily lives of the German people. Even those who hated Joseph Stalin acknowledged that he worked 16 hours a day. 2s also need to be on guard about taking on more than they can handle, which is a form of delusion. They can be drawn into responsibility overload when the façade number is a 4, 8, or 9. Of all the 2s, someone born on the 2nd is most likely to be able to talk himself into or out of a situation, providing he doesn't get flustered by the stress of the moment.

The 2 Birthday also thinks well on his feet if he is acclimated to whatever situation he is working with. The aggressive nature of the number 9 pushing the more laid-back 2 makes a 29 Birthday the type who often takes on more than he wants or gets into difficult situations they regret. This tendency, coupled with the 2's inclination toward self-delusion can make for especially devastating effects. President John Kennedy twice ordered the Pentagon to remove intercontinental ballistic missiles from Turkey that threatened the Soviet Union, and he didn't understand why the military ignored the order. In spite of his worldliness, he never fully understood the limitations of his office in the general scheme of the political structure.

2s have a basic challenge that applies to Libra: maintaining balance in their lives. This especially applies to people born on the 11th. Some numerologists see an 11 Birthday as more spiritually inclined or intuitive than all other numbers. In everyday life, I've seen 11 Birthday numbers to be the most indecisive and scattered. This scattered mindset often is the cause of the 2 transposing letters, numbers, and words, and also being "repetitively redundant." The tendency to transpose in some 2s become as strong as to make them wonder if they suffer from dyslexia, even when there is no clinical basis to believe so. They can deal with this tendency by avoiding being in a hurry. Speaking of being in a hurry, 2 Birthdays are the procrastinators of the world, yet they make it seem as though they aren't putting things off. They just never believe they are ready for whatever they need to do.

Being the diplomats they are, they will have all sorts of reasons for not getting on with business. It is the other person who must understand. This is why the 2's romantic partner needs to be more decisive and definitive. Mental illness strikes all the numbers, but such a condition would be especially difficult for the already very emotional 2.

With the sun and moon being the providers of light in different forms of life-giving energy, a 2/1 marriage would work best if the 2 is the female, and she understands that the male wouldn't want the traditional role of wearing the pants in the family. A 1 will lead the relationship. In the worst scenario, the 1 easily could dominate the relationship, with the 2's only real trump card being it stubbornness and capability for denial. She definitely would have to live with the 1's tendency to be aloof. He would be able to offer emotional support for only short periods.

The perpetual challenge for a 2 Birthday is to realize that your nurturing isn't always appreciated or wanted. This makes the 2 frustrated and increases the drive to find the individual who will appreciate that giving side. Finding that appreciative someone won't satisfy the strong need for approval. The 2 dislikes, even hates, making up one's mind and sticking with a decision.

A couple of 2s can be friends, but not roommates or long-term romantic partners. Both of them need maximum personal space at the end of the day. Each likes to be pursued. One or both of them, probably the female, soon would become tired of chasing. A 2 Birthday man might be a bit too laid back for many women and might be the type of man that a woman has to lead by the ear because he would be too indecisive and noncommittal. 2s might not make the best romantic couples, yet they continue to attract each other.

Chapter 13: The Zodiac

You've probably used horoscopes before, perhaps in the back of a popular magazine or online. These simple astrological reviews are based on the twelve signs of the zodiac. Horoscopes draw vague, and often fun, conclusions about a person's life based on what sign in the zodiac the sun was positioned in when they were born. These practices are relatively simple, but the zodiac is much more complex than general assumptions about one's love life.

From our perspective here on earth, the zodiac is a path that the sun travels across the sky. As he travels, he passes through twelve different sections of the sky each one with a constellation of stars that also appear to move across the sky in the opposite direction. The constellations are as follows starting with the sun's 'home' in Aries then; Taurus, Gemini, Cancer, Leo, Virgo, Libra, Scorpio, Sagittarius, Capricorn, Aquarius, and Pisces. After this, we return to Aries. All planets in our solar system are moving within the sphere of these constellations respectively.

Although from our perspective it may seem like the heavens are moving around the earth, but we know now that the earth itself is moving around the sun. These patterns create a dance in the sky, and when studied can lead to correlated patterns to events on earth. And although many popular horoscopes are based around where the sun is positioned, all the other planets have influence over other parts of our lives creating a quite complicated equation.

The zodiac has become a household term in the western world ever since the influx of horoscope astrology and other celestial practices became popular in the 1970s. Although the ideas and use of the zodiac are centuries old, it has only been used in popular culture since its rise in popularity in the past few decades. Let's explore its history and use.

The Signs

Each of the twelve signs of the zodiac has their own distinct set of traits. Each one comes equipped with a sigil, an animal image, color, number, planetary ruler, element, part of the human body, and many other personality traits that make the sign unique. With the study of these signs, we not only learn about the nature of reality itself but also of our true nature depending on the sign's influence over our lives.

Most popular horoscopes are written using the Sun sign only. Although where the sun is placed in the chart is very important, it is not the only planetary influence that needs to be considered. Horoscopes can be fun and give a broad insight into sun influence if written well, but to get the most out of astrology, we need to learn about all the signs and the planets placed within them in our natal chart. This being said, we need to keep in mind that no person is purely an Aries or Taurus; all the signs play a role in influencing your life. Even if there is no planet in a certain sign in your natal chart, there will typically be a transit or aspect in those signs at some point in your life.

Below we will list the signs and give a broad overview of what area of life the sign governs. Each sign has its own unique influence over certain behaviors, this plus the influence and support form houses and of course planets creates a complex combination of influences. Study these signs and make it a point to follow the sun or moon through these signs on a daily basis, this will help you get to know them and learn their personalities so you may better work with them throughout your life.

Aries

Ram – Cardinal Fire – Ruler: Mars

Aries is considered the first astrological month and begins right after the spring equinox. This lengthening of daylight is fitting for fiery Aries, the sun is making its way to exaltation and will exalt in another fire sign, Leo. The goat is used as the animal image for Aries since the Aries influence is energetic and always needing to move. Courageous and full of life, Aries is competitive and absolutely loves to win. Leadership roles and creative ways of solving problems are other Aries influences. As with other fire signs, Aries is impatient but warm, impulsive and excitable, and yet the optimistic approach to life is very welcoming at times. Spontaneous fits of temper are common for Aries but never lasts too long, Aries is very forgivable and never remains sad or angry for long periods of time.

Taurus

Bull – Fixed Earth – Ruler: Venus

The Taurus influence is patient and peaceful, but when excited can be very assertive. Relaxed at most times, the Taurus influence enjoys sensual pleasures especially food and viewing beautiful artwork or music. Stability and comfort are a must for Taurus to be happy and he's more than content to put in some hard work to achieve his creature comforts. If excited this sign is best avoided, not unlike an actual bull, you do not want to be on the receiving end of his temper. Rural areas are favored by Taurus; cities tend to be anxious and fast-paced, not his favorite atmosphere. While this influence offers talents in art and craftsmanship, some may find it difficult to decide on a career path; the calm bull is in no hurry to make decisions. Reliability and a firm foundation come along with this earth sign's demeanor.

Gemini

Twins – Mutable air – Ruler: Mercury

Gemini has a tendency to offer talents in writing and teaching. The image of the twins is very fitting since Gemini loves to share with others. Communication is a key influence from the twins and this is often manifested as a caring and open personality. Curiosity and a general interest in everything, Gemini loves to chat with friends or acquaintances about any topic. Being alone is not favored by the Gemini influence; this makes for a healthy social life and large friend circles. Knowledge on a variety of topics makes Gemini influenced people very fun to be around; they are very engaging and can find a way to connect very easily. Typically, up to date on current trends and culture, Gemini enjoys discussing art, politics and world events. Traveling and exploring new cultures is a must for the Gemini.

Cancer

Crab – Cardinal Water – Ruler: Moon

The influence of Cancer is mirrored by the behavior of crabs. Its home is wherever he is and if need be, he can cling very tightly to something he wants. This is common behavior for Cancer influenced people, often moving from home to home and being stubborn if he can't get his way. Cancers are family-oriented but tend to be passive in communication, often going out of their way to avoid confrontation. Family and relationships are coveted by cancer and he desperately tries to not lose any friends or family by trying to please them even if he may disagree or not want to directly confront the situation. The behavior of Cancer can be very needy, requiring lots of attention and confirmation from loved ones. They need security to compensate for their passive and sensitive approach to life. Although often reserved, when relaxed Cancer can be very fun loving and talented, with a deep insight that comes along with the support of the water element.

Leo

Lion – Fixed Fire – Ruler: Sun

The influence of Leo is proud and energetic; this sign offers a sense of dignity and confidence. The Lion is an obvious match for this sign; the king of the jungle knows what he wants and knows how to get it. All aspects of Leo are confident, communication, demeanor and even appearances can invoke confidence.

Although serious and balanced the lion enjoys relaxation and playfulness as well. This makes for a combination that is perfect for careers that require leadership or performance. Leo loves attention and often can be cranky if their desire for it isn't fulfilled. Little tasks and mundane events are of no concern for Leos; they predominantly of the big picture and do not like being bossed around. Leo is always seeking love and attention, always checking to see if they are being watched, and hoping for approval from an outside perspective. Leo may present an overly self-involved influence; it is important for people with heavy Leo placement to realize that while they love the attention, other people need some love also.

Virgo

Maiden – Mutable Earth – Ruler: Mercury

The influence of Virgo is clear-headedness and the ability to be as one pointed as necessary. Virgo is gentle and soft-spoken, with a quiet demeanor that may seem like shyness, but typically isn't the case. The thoughtful maiden is usually contemplating or listening rather than avoiding the situation. They love crafts and are willing to work hard to create beauty through artistic endeavor. This quiet and craft attitude is perfect for being alone, and Virgo spends her time alone wisely. While being alone is fine for the maiden, she also wishes to contribute to society in meaningful ways. Service jobs and charitable causes are ideal for Virgo to ensure that their time alone isn't consuming their life. This balance is the lesson of Virgo. The Earth element contributes to this selfless mindset. Earth signs love to help others as much as possible.

Libra

Scales – Cardinal Air – Ruler: Venus

The influence of Libra is symbolized by a set of scales for a reason, Libra values balance and aims to create balance every moment throughout life. Work versus play is a big struggle for many people and Libra knows how to balance these two perfectly. Libra can also see the balance of positivity and negativity in everyday life, knowing that happiness is not possible without sadness. This balanced mindset may make it tough for Libra to make decisions; this is a result of being able to quickly weigh the positive and negative sides of any given situation. The focus on harmony is great for the Libra in relationships, striving for balance; they know how to handle emotional situations and find the balance within them. Libra will not tolerate a one-sided relationship and cannot put up with not being appreciated. Libras love art and prefer harmonious music as compared to dissonance or disruptive themes. Science and mathematics are appealing to Libra since there is a solidly constructed rulebook for these practices. The Air element adds to the love of harmony as well, the 'floating on air' feeling when everything is perfectly balanced.

Scorpio

Scorpion – Fixed Water – Ruler: Pluto

The influence of Scorpio offers behavior that is contemplative and serious. He needs time to think deeply about things before he acts; this allows him to be meticulous and focused. Not unlike an actual scorpion, Scorpio can be dangerous if angered or betrayed. Don't be fooled by Scorpio's shy and quiet demeanor; he is intense and very good at deception or learning secrets. He can see through other people's deception very easily and knows how to understand their deceit. Scorpio is not easily frightened; they defend themselves and their loved ones with assertion and fortitude. Scorpio seeks justice in all areas of life; his deep thought offers much time to analyze society and the injustices within. The intense depth of thought also leads Scorpio to influence our lives in a way that requires us to understand our true selves. People with a heavy Scorpio influence spend a lot of time analyzing their past actions and the present effects of the actions. Careers that require seriousness and deep studies are suitable for Scorpio, surgeons, psychiatry and other healing careers are perfect. As a water sign Scorpio offers a heightened sensitivity as well, so tread lightly not to anger him.

Sagittarius

Centaur – Mutable Fire – Ruler: Jupiter

The influence of Sagittarius is adventurous and social. This optimistic sign is symbolized by the Centaur, a mythological creature that is half man and half horse. This creature roams the earth on adventures simply seeking joy and new experience. The Centaur carries a bow and arrow; this is symbolic of choosing goals and attaining them. Imagine the centaur firing his arrow, only to chase it down and shoot again. This pursuit of adventurous goals is personified in people who have a heavy Sagittarian influence. This adventurous spirit requires a nomadic attitude and plenty of freedom. If Sagittarius is not free to do as he pleases, then he is left unfulfilled and distressed. The desire to keep moving is not only physical but mental as well. Some may find themselves unable to finish projects before starting new ones, leaving many goals unattended too. This is the lesson of Sagittarius, to complete what you started. World culture and athletics are of much interest to Sagittarius; they love playing and having fun in general. Sagittarius is an obvious Fire sign, travel and constant movement are required for fulfillment, while confidence guides the way.

Capricorn

Goat-mermaid – Cardinal Earth – Ruler: Saturn

The influence of Capricorn is filled with structure and logic. This Saturn ruled sign is serious and goal oriented. The mountain goat is the symbolic image for Capricorn, not only a goat but also a mermaid; this is curious as a mythological creature associated with death and the underworld. Capricorn is self-disciplined and supports boundaries and restrictions in the form of goals and desired achievement. The Capricorn influence offers skills in craftsmanship and overall any line of work that requires hard work. A career in law or politics is favorable for Capricorn. Diplomacy and reason are attributed to this sign as well. The use of well thought out tactics and defense are common among those with heavy Capricorn influence; they tend to be tough to read and rarely let their guards down. With the Earth influence Capricorn is equipped with a level head and great family skills, often the voice of reason during dramatic family events.

Aquarius

Water bearer – Fixed Air – Ruler: Uranus

The influence of Aquarius is genuinely concerned for the well-being of others. Aquarius readily offers gifts to those in need and happily would give their last drop of water to someone rather than drink it themselves. This selflessness and lack of prejudice is the lesson of Aquarius, trying not to exhaust themselves by attempting to help everyone all the time. The friendly and clever Aquarius may be excellent inventors and love new technological gadgetry. They may even be involved in politics, offering their sense of justice and genuine love of people as a means of diplomacy. Aquarius is empathetic as well, offering a heightened ability to sense the feelings of others. Aquarius does not judge others by their appearances and gives the benefit of the doubt in most situations. This water bearer is happy to nourish the world with much-needed waters, often in the form of a charitable cause or a simple, friendly smile.

Pisces

Fish – Mutable Water – Ruler: Neptune

The influence of Pisces is graceful and secretive. The mysteries of the ocean and its beautiful rhythm makes the fish a suitable image for the Pisces attitude.

Pisces loves the arts, especially art with esoteric themes and abstract ideas that can be interpreted any number of ways. Their private internal reality is rarely shared with others; they hold their secrets dear and are not concerned with impressing others with their valuable perspective. Pisces enjoys helping the downtrodden, often going out of their way to cheer someone up with a joke or fun gesture. Pisces is often misunderstood due to the secrecy of their inner dialogue; this can lead to trouble making connections with others. Their knowledge of the mysteries of life and natural magic are often seen as ridiculous and can push away some of the more skeptical types of people. Pisces is very loving and sometimes can find a way to securely share their inner dialogue through writing or artistic endeavors. Imaginative and open to the mysterious nature of the world, Pisces holds important gifts that are attainable you are trustworthy and humble.

Chapter 14: Personal Day

The personal day number provides insight into the ebb and flow of our lives on a day to day basis. The numbers reveal tendencies for certain types of things to exist or happen.

Generate a numerology personal day calendar further below.

Master numbers will be published on the calendar when relevant. Read about how to determine when a master number is a master number. In essence, when the life path number or at least one of the three major name numbers is a master number then printing the master numbers on the personal day calendar is relevant.

Each personal day calendar generation is for one calendar month. Up to 12 individual calendar months of personal day numbers can be generated.

The interpretations below the calendar are a synopsis of the tendencies or resonance most likely to be present for certain personal day numbers.

The interpretations also may be consulted to determine the best personal day number for special occasions or other events or plans that have personal significance. When the number is determined, the personal day calendar can be consulted to see which days will have that personal day number.

What Is a Personal Day Number?

The Personal Day Number in numerology shows that you have to be aware and careful since the things done on this day will lay the foundation for the days to come.

The work you do, your thoughts during the day will set the platform for the days to come. Youwill have to pay close attention to the activities of the day. If you are wondering how to calculate personal day number, try this free numerology calculator now! And then let's take a look at the personal day number meanings from 1 to 9.

Personal Day Number Meanings

Personal Day Number 1

This is the day when your primary concern is about yourself, your personal goals and desires. You have some innovative and original ideas which you would like to put to good use. This is also a time when you are vulnerable to the negative influences of others. You should be confident on your own abilities and work on your own to achieve success. This numerology number will analyze your dreams, wants and desires.

Personal Day Number 2

This is the day to be social and develop a friendly relationship with others. You like to be in the company of friends. Try to resolve differences with others. You don't like to dominate and be dominated in any case.

Personal Day Number 3

The numerology reading for this number shows that you will get fun from some lively recreational activities on this day. You like to enjoy the small joys that life has to offer on this day. Make the most of it and don't let worries to overcome you. It is the perfect day for some fun and enjoyment. You need to be busy, engage in recreational activities. You will be very communicative. You will have to be careful about your conversation with others.

Personal Day Number 4

This is the day of maximum hard work and success in your business affairs. You should cherish the fruitful results generated by your hard work. The 4 Personal Day is to make every labour you put as fruitful as you can. It is an auspicious day to settle business dealings. You should be proud of everything you do today.

Personal Day Number 5

On this day you would love to travel to distant places for relaxation. This is a day to make good and valuable friendships. This is a day when you are raring to move ahead in life with new energy and vigour. You will face changes, renovation; engage in tours on this day. This is the day to make some good friends.

Personal Day Number 6

According to numerology predictions, this is a day to maintain balance and harmony in life. This istime to spend some quality time with your friends and family. Your main concern should be about your family and domestic matters. It is the number that brings balance to our lives, you will feel a need to seek out and create harmony in every possible way. This is a good time when you should look for the happiness of your family and friends. This is an auspicious time to buy a house, spend time with family and friends.

Personal Day Number 7

There is a tendency to lose your calm and feel disturbed on this personal day 7. You should try to avoid conflicts and maintain a calm and composed demeanour throughout. Make an extra effort to stay calm and composed throughout the day. There is a tendency to get upset, confused and frustrated soon. You should avoid it.

Personal Day Number 8

This is a day to take some important professional decisions in life. Business and financial decisions taken on this day would reap good results. This is the day when you will be successful in whatever you do. You are able to make quick decisions since you are full of positive energies on this day.

Personal Day Number 9

The number 9 personal day is a day to cherish the companionship of others. This is a day of caring and sharing. You get great joy in sharing your achievements with others. You share with others gladly and without reservation. This is not the day to start new ventures. Instead, spend time with your near ones.

Chapter 15: Personality Number

Your personality number is made up of the consonants in your name (the letters that aren't vowels, so don't include Y or W in your calculation if you have used them when calculating your soul number).

The consonants refer to the outer world and the first impression you make on it. It describes how others may see you. Additionally, this number relates to your inner desires and your fantasies. These may or may not be realised during your lifetime.

You dream of being a leader. You want to be recognised for your courage, daring, and original ideas. You often come over as aggressive and very sure of yourself. You do best when allowed your own ideas. Beware of being selfish or melodramatic.

You dream of a meaningful relationship. You are easy going and encourage cooperation. Aware of others' needs, you try to show friendliness, understanding and tact. You may be artistic and are likely to be shy. Your life may contain many ups and downs. Beware of being grasping, over protective or cranky.

You dream of expressing yourself artistically. You tend to learn through experience. You want to be popular and appreciated and therefore strive to uplift and colour your surroundings. Beware of being pessimistic and foolhardy.

You dream of being someone people can depend on. You want to be seen as someone who has a plan and the discipline to make it work. You are constructive, realistic, traditional and cautious and direct your energy towards achieving your goals. You can be a loner, but are always straightforward and reliable. Beware of being boring.

You dream of being unrestrained by responsibility. You see yourself conversing and mingling with people from many different places, living for adventure.

Although you have the ability to think critically, sometimes you over-think things. You are constantly asking questions and can be highly persuasive. Beware of being unreliable.

You dream of the perfect family. Stability is important to you. Sometimes you can be opinionated and anxious if you feel insecure. You might take on the burdens of others unnecessarily. Although you possess charm and grace, sometimes you can be disloyal and vengeful. Beware of being jealous and bitter.

You dream of being a shutting yourself away from the world to study. You may be eccentric or a loner. As you operate on a different wavelength to most people, you can be difficult to understand as well as get to know. You are happy to ask questions, but less so to answer them. Analysing everything can create a distance between you and others. Being afraid of betrayal makes you hold people at a distance. Beware of being deceptive and insincere.

You dream of political or business success. You crave authority and recognition. Tending to be formal, stern, and hard-headed, you're most comfortable in the realm of tangible facts. Money and material success are important to you as is your reputation. Beware of being too materialistic.

You dream of being a selfless humanitarian. You are most at home in the realm of the arts, medicine, religion, drama, philosophy and metaphysics. You tend to act for the benefit of others and seek solutions from the inspirational, intuitive and creative worlds. You would like to someone that people count on for support and advice. Beware of being unrealistic.

You dream of being a true idealist. You have plenty of inner wisdom and charisma. A dreamer, you have a visionary outlook and artistic sensitivity and a sparkling quality. You have a unique perspective and philosophy. At times you may appear unstable and can seem distant and detached. You believe there is more to life than we can know or prove. Beware of being impractical.

You dream of changing the world. You seek to bring together the people and resources you need to make your dreams reality. You may seem ahead of your time as you are quick witted, far-sighted and intuitive, interested in anything new or revolutionary. Your high idealism makes you want the best for everyone and you are full of big ideas. Beware of wasting your potential.

You dream of raising social consciousness and becoming a master teacher and healer. Your fantasy is to focus all your energies and abilities towards the good of others. You also want to find full understanding and wisdom before preaching to others. Beware of lacking personal ambition.

BIRTHDAY NUMBER

The day of the month you were born on is connected to your talents and abilities (especially those you are comfortable with), and the type of career you are likely to be suited to. It also describes how you go about meeting your obligations. Its greatest influence tends to be between the ages of about 28 and 56. Your birthday number is a good reflection of how you about performing your duties.

No calculations are needed for this number. Simply note the meaning of the date of the month on which you were born. (Although you do not need to reduce this number, it does have a relationship with its root number.)

You have a dynamic personality and are often the centre of attention. You have will power, self-confidence and tend to ignore details in favour of a broader approach. You may be more of a leader than your life path indicates. Although sensitive, you tend to hide your feelings.

Career: Independent or in a leading role. Arts, working with children, animals or pets.

Intuitive, you relate emotionally rather than intellectually. Your compassionate side prompts you to look after others. Personal contact is important to you and you make friends easily. Warm-hearted, you constantly seek affection. Too many people around you can make you nervous. Beware of becoming depressed or moody. You may be more emotional and sensitive than your life path indicates.

Career: As part of a team. Care work, looking after others.

You understand those different to yourself and are able to assimilate complex issues. Able to bounce back rapidly from setbacks, you are restless. You have good communication skills and a good imagination. Beware of scattering your energies. You are affectionate, but sometimes over- sensitive. You may be able to bounce back more quickly from setbacks than your life path indicates.

Career: Writing, speaking, singing, travel, education, publishing.

You have a lot of energy and like to be in control. Sincere and honest, you are serious and hard working. Beware of repressing your feelings. You may be better organised and more responsible than your life path indicates.

Career: Working alone, management.

You have an inquisitive mind and explore new ideas in an analytical way. You work well with people and are versatile. Change is important to you and your mind is quick, clever and analytical. Beware of becoming bored and shirking your responsibilities. You may be more curious and welcome new ideas more easily than your life path indicates.

Career: Working with others, travel. Anything where you perform a service or need to think quickly.

You can make friends easily and your sense of diplomacy means that you always know what to say. You are responsible, helpful and understanding with a high level of concern for others. You may be more responsible and helpful than your life path indicates.

Career: Any profession that allows you to express your love of beauty or develop relationships.

You are idealistic and feel let down when others don't live according to your expectations. You are good at mental analysis and complicated reasoning. You can be emotional and intuitive. Beware of being self-centred and stubborn. You may be more of a perfectionist than your life path indicates.

Career: Working alone, management. Medicine, cosmetic industry.

Your serious approach means you honour your commitments. You like to use your organisational skills and can conceive and plan on a grand scale. You're a good judge of values and very reliable with money. You're never too busy to spend time on worthwhile causes. You may be more business minded than your life path indicates.

Career: Running your own business, commerce, executive, banking, finance.

You are an independent thinker and are broadminded, tolerant and generous as well as sensitive to others' needs and feelings. Your feelings run deep and you often find yourself in dramatically charged situations. You may be more of a humanitarian than your life path indicates.

Career: Working with people, IT, charity work.

You can channel your intensity to accomplish your goals. Although you have a sunny disposition, beware of going to extremes and over-dominating situations. You have will power and self-confidence with an original approach and a compelling manner. You may be more of a leader than your life path indicates.

Career: Working independently or in a leading role. Arts, medicine, working with children, animals or pets.

You are sensitive and can pick up on people's emotional states which you may confuse for your own. Beware of becoming too emotionally involved. You have a talent for persuasion and are an idealist, a dreamer rather than a doer. You may be more emotional and sensitive than your life path indicates.

Career: Working with the public, public relations, caring.

You often have to finish projects others have begun. You can be restless, but your mind is practical and rational. You possess wisdom that only your closest friends are aware of because you don't tend to express your opinions or give advice. You can be affectionate, but are subject to ups and downs. You may be able to bounce back more quickly from setbacks than your life path indicates.

Career: Teaching, sales, writing.

You can see things through to completion. You are persuasive and intense manner and may intimidate the less confident. You are hardworking and sincere in all your efforts. Beware of intolerance. You may be better organised and more responsible than your life path indicates.

Career: Working alone, management.

You are methodical and try to carve out a niche to enable you to work independently. You have a quick, clever and analytical mind. Able to pay close attention to detail, you are good at presenting ideas. Beware of becoming bored and shirking responsibility. You may be more curious and welcome new ideas more easily than your life path indicates.

Career: Working with people. Administrative, managerial.

Responsible and capable, you prefer a harmonious environment and tend to learn by observation. You are strongly attached to your home and family. You can be generous and giving person, but beware of being stubborn. You may have artistic talents. You may be more responsible and helpful than your life path indicates.

Career: Teacher, diplomat, mediator.

As an idealist, you can buck the system in an effort to bring about what you believe to be needed change. Most of your actions are born from logic, responsibility and a rational approach. You seek unusual approaches and are relatively inflexible. Beware of being too introspective. You may be more idealistic than your life path indicates.

Career: Technical, scientific, religious, charity work, with water.

You learn through experience. With your sympathetic disposition, you can relate well with people from all walks of life. You are fortunate financially and are ambitious and goal oriented. Beware of starting things and not finishing them. You may be more business minded than your life path indicates.

Career: Running your own business, commerce, executive, banking, finance, sales.

You are sensitive and tend to use your intuition to help you succeed. Beware of working with people who try to discredit you and being over dramatic. Inspiring innovation, you are suited to roles that require problem solving and change management. You may be more of a humanitarian than your life path indicates.

Career: Working with others, administration.

You are sensitive and have a compelling manner that can dominate many situations. You don't tend to follow convention or take advice very well. You tend to learn through experience. You may be more nervous and prone to anger than your life path indicates.

Career: IT, any form of technology.

You are warm-hearted and have an emotional understanding that constantly seeks affection. You are receptive but beware of going to extremes in your reactions and becoming depressed or moody. Highly sociable, you make friends easily and quickly. You may be more emotional and sensitive than your life path indicates.

Career: Caring for others.

You are level headed and usually complete what you have begun. You express yourself well and are able to make a good impression. You have a keen imagination, but tend to scatter your energies. You may bounce back more quickly from setbacks than your life path indicates.

Career: Speculative ventures, publishing, advisory roles.

You are able to use your intuition. Hidden enemies can make your life complicated if they discover your weaknesses.keywordsYour approach can be unorthodox but you are capable of handling large-scale undertakings, assuming responsibility, and working long and hard. Beware of being sloppy about details. You may be better organised and more responsible than your life path indicates.

Career: Architecture, homemaking, organisational skills.

You are analytical and question the world around you. You are talented and versatile and good at presenting ideas. You tend to need change and travel. Beware of becoming impatient and shirking responsibility. You may be more curious and welcome new ideas more easily than your life path indicates.

Career: Programmer, accountant, clerical, mediator.

You are pleasant, though forceful, and can get what you want out of life. You are responsible and put a lot of effort into your relationships and have many friends. You are devoted to your family. Beware of being too forceful. You may be more responsible and helpful than your life path indicates.

Career: Law, mediator, helping others.

There is a spiritual side to your nature, which you express only to your closest friends. You are a perfectionist and a stickler for details. Your thinking is logical and intuitive, rational and responsible. Beware of becoming depressed if things don't go your way. You may be more idealistic than your life path indicates.

Career: Counsellor, healer.

You tend to be serious and are a hard worker with organisational skills You are efficient and can handle money well. You are conscientious and deal well with responsibility. Generally sociable and diplomatic, you tend to use persuasion rather than force. You may be more business minded than your life path indicates.

Career: Managerial, executive, administrative, work with money.

You are intelligent and prefer to surround yourself with like-minded people. You can work well with people, but also need time alone. You tend to use persuasion rather than force to achieve your ends. Beware of being fickle. You may be more of a humanitarian than your life path indicates.

Career: Science, telecommunications or research.

You see yourself as a star and can feel threatened by those who you see as more skilled than yourself. You will work hard for results. You have plenty of will power and self-confidence, and often a rather original approach. You are able to start a job and continue until it's finished.keywordsBeware of being too dominating. You may be more of a leader than your life path indicates.

Career: Working with others, any creative field.

You are imaginative and creative, with intuitive skills and analytical abilities. Beware of overreacting when under pressure. Nervous tension can be a problem for you. You may be more emotional and sensitive than your life path indicates.keywords

Career: Being responsible for others, not in the business world.

Knowledgeable, you are able to confidently converse on many different subjects. Education is important to you. You have a good way of expressing yourself with words. Beware of always thinking you're right and scattering your energies. You may bounce back more quickly from setbacks than your life path indicates.

Career: Education, academia, publishing, travel.

Others follow your lead because they can sense your inner strength and confidence. Serious and sincere, you have the patience and determination necessary to accomplish a great deal. Although you are practical, you have a good imagination. Beware of being rigid and stubborn and scattering your energy. You may be better organised and more responsible than your life path indicates.

Chapter 16: What About Changed Names

You may have questions related to name change and the effect it has on your destiny, success and so on. You now know that all calculation centers on your official name only but what about the name you adopt in marriage, your day-to-day business, friendships, professions and in public life.

Change of names may be permanent like in marriage or temporary like a childhood nickname or acting name. Most of us have been addressed in different names in the course of life, which have sometimes stuck in our lives all through. Obviously, sometimes you might pick a name or nickname unaware of the vibration it produces but sometimes stage names and pen names are carefully selected in order to help you achieve your desired destiny. Did you know that changed names could interfere with your destiny in a similar manner as that of your birth name? You should realize that every name you use in your lifetime has its own special meaning.

For example, if you have a name with a destiny number 2 and you change to a name expressing different qualities like number 8, you will definitely have changed your destiny and personality. The changed name will somehow mask the real you. Changing your name can also cause an imbalance on your numerology profile. For instance, if your life path number is 5 and your date of birth is 23rd, which also has the 5 energy, if you take on a name that has another 5 energy, you will be burdened by the presence of the extra number. Overemphasis of any number in a profile greatly manifests negative characteristics associated with the number. In this case, you may become more irresponsible, careless, and rebellious when using this changed name.

To understand more on the name you are thinking of changing to or the changed name you are currently using and what it portrays about you, calculate its numerological value using the methods that you learnt earlier then check on the meaning of the number you come up with.

In addition, be careful when selecting names of your future babies in case you have them. Consider subjecting your choices to numerological calculation before you give your baby a name, to minimize any tendencies you don't want to see in your child. That said, even the nicknames should be watched with a close eye.

Chapter 17: Breaking Down The Expression Number Further

Expression numbers show the personality and ability of one person. This may also reveal one's talents and shortcomings that may enter his/her life. The numbers associated with your name reveals your development while you are working out some issues and making the most of your talents. For those who believe in reincarnation, numerology may also work that way. Your full name's vibration is seen in the totality of your development which may include experiences, wisdom you accumulated, and talents. Every experience, whether big or small can influence your life. The expression is not a prediction or something that you may use in the future, but it is a way on how to know your personality and ability. With the use of expression number, you will understand your personality and nature.

Importance of Expression Number

Some people view Expression numbers as just a piece of advice. But, what they don't know is that, this might help them develop their skills and talents in the future. The meanings of these numbers can also be the best way to get rid of your weakness and to balance it with your strength. If you don't know how to calculate your expression, try knowing the corresponding numbers of your name. Then, add them. Whatever the outcome is, that is your personality or talent. Some say that expression numbers are just coincidence. However, according to numerologists, the birth name of a person is not a coincidence, but it is meant for them. So, this means that the calculations and your name have nothing to do with your expression number. If you can't still figure out on how to calculate, then seek a good source of information. You may conduct online research or use some magazines that revolve around expression number. Or, if you know a numerologist, you may ask him or her for some help. It is because numerologists know different things about numbers and they can guide you when making decisions.

Chapter 18: Six Of Wands

The Six of Wands illustrates a victorious man holding a wand adorned with a laurel wreath and parading on a white horse. The laurel wreath in the ancient Greek culture marks him as a man of triumph, competent, honored and confident. The white horse represents strength, purity, and the success of an adventure. He is accompanied by applauding footmen with wands signifying acknowledgement of victory particularly on a public level. It is a pure physical victory that has been gained unlike a spiritual one as in the Sun card it does stop them from enjoying the momentary pleasure and acclaim. Every victory need not necessarily be a spiritual one. Everyone likes heaven, but no one likes to die. This card promises the deserved public acclamation at international level for your leadership, talents, drive and uniqueness to the natives who fall under the influence of this number. However, it is up to them to put in sincere efforts in all their endeavors. Also they should make sure that they do not succeed at the expense of others and become a cause for dishonor.

Chanakya

Name Number 28

Chanakya was a teacher to the first Mauryan Emperor Chandragupta who lived in the third century BC. Traditionally, Chanakya is also identified by the name Kautilya (name number 28), who pioneered and authored the ancient Indian economic and political treatise called Arthasastra. In the Western world, he has been referred to as The Indian Machiavelli, although Chanakya's works predate Machiavelli's by about 1,800 years. Chanakya was insulted and thrown out of the Nanda Kingdom in his early age. Later he worked a teacher in Taksashila, an ancient centre of learning, where he came across a boy called Chandragupta whom he mentored. Chandragupta later avenged his mentor's insult by overthrowing the Nanda king and established the Mauryan dynasty, the first of its kind on the Indian subcontinent. Chanakya's magnum opus works were rediscovered in 1915.

Hegel

Name Number 28

Georg Wilhelm Friedrich Hegel popularly known as Hegel is regarded as one of the creators of German idealism. He revolutionized European philosophy and was an important precursor to Marxism. Hegel's concept explains that mind and spirit manifested itself in a set of contradictions that are integrated without eliminating either pole or reducing one to the other.

One simple example of such contradiction is immanence and transcendence pair that is used primarily with reference to God's relation to the world. Transcendent means that God is completely outside of and beyond the world, as contrasted with immanence the notion that God is manifested in the world.

SEVEN OF WANDS

The Seven of Wands is depicted by a young man in green dress who defends himself with one wand against 6 others with a deep emotion in his eyes. He wears one boot and one shoe and stands on the high ground. People who fall under the influence of this master number achieve their desired goal, but the rewards are at risk of being seized by one or more opponents. Others may feel jealous of their accomplishment. The natives must continually struggle to maintain their position. The man in green attire symbolizes abundance, fertility and prosperity and water that is flowing under his feet is a symbolism of dreams and emotions. It's presence in the seven of wands indicates that a deeply trenched emotional investment is required. The odd combination of shoe and a boot that the man wears is not conventional. Eccentricity in a positive light can be described creative genius on the higher octave and creative madness in the lower octave. So, here eccentricity is perfectly acceptable as long as no one is being hurt. Those under the influence of this number can expect big challenges in their business and personal life. They will require honesty, courage and high enthusiasm to defend what is rightfully yours. Beware of being a martyr.

Muhammad

Name Number 29

Muhammad is the founder of the religion of Islam and is considered by Muslims to be a messenger and prophet of God. He was also active as a social reformer, diplomat, merchant, philosopher, orator, legislator, military leader, humanitarian, philanthropist, and, according to Muslim belief, an agent of divine action. Muhammad gained few followers early on, and was met with hostility from some Meccan tribes. In Medina, Muhammad united the conflicting tribes, and after eight years of fighting with the Meccan tribes, his followers, who by then had grown to 10,000, conquered Mecca. In

632, a few months after returning to Medina from his Farewell pilgrimage, Muhammad fell ill and died. By the time of his death, most of the Arabian Peninsula had converted to Islam, and he had united the tribes of Arabia into a single Muslim religious polity.

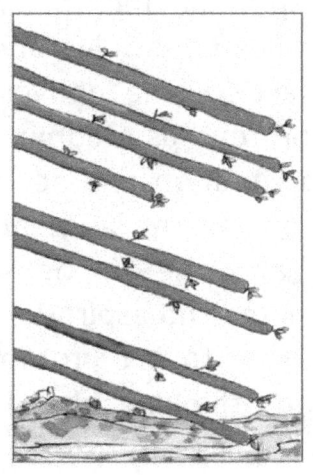

EIGHT OF WANDS

The Eight of Wands does not display any people or characters. Instead, it shows a flight of eight wands swiftly moving towards its destination in a focused direction and structure. In the background, the beautiful landscape with a fertile valley, river, mountain and clear sky signifies perfect weather conditions. The Eight of Wands itself is a symbol of triumph caused by incidental circumstances. It is a perfect card of hope that promises a bright future. There will be growth in spiritual, mental and physical planes. Advancement in life and work may come too fast for the natives to handle and it can be read as a command to take charge of a situation and act swiftly. The clear skies and warm landscape are only temporary, and the timing is right for pursuing dreams and aspirations. Failure is likely if you fail to act promptly or over react without thinking ahead. This card rules over quick transformations and changes similar to the Tower Card. The native's ideal job may be one that requires quick thought and undeviated focus. Possible categories would be: emergency healthcare, Traffic Controllers, Military, Financial/Investment, Politics, and Law Enforcement among others. The key is to look for positions which will keep you active and busy; otherwise you might have a tendency to become bored.

Patanjali

Name Number 30

Patanjali is the compiler of the Yoga Sutras, an important collection of aphorisms on Yoga practice in 150 BCE. In recent decades the Yoga Sutra has become quite popular worldwide. "Yoga" in traditional Hinduism involves inner contemplation, a system of meditation practice

Mozart

Name Number 30

Mozart was a prolific and influential composer of the classical era and is among the most enduringly popular of classical composers. Mozart learned voraciously from others, and developed a brilliance and maturity of style that encompassed the light and graceful along with the dark and passionate. His influence on subsequent Western art music is profound. Beethoven also wrote his own early compositions in the shadow of Mozart.

Jamsetji Tata

Name Number 30

Jamsetji Tata was an Indian entrepreneur and industrialist, prominent for his pioneering work in Indian industry. He founded what would later become the Tata Group and is today among the largest and most respected companies of the world. Jamsetji was a pioneer in his field. He is regarded as the "Father of Indian industry". Jamshedpur city was renamed as Tatanagar in his honor.

NINE OF WANDS

The Nine of Wands depicts a tired, injured man who holds a wand to defend his freedom of expression. His posture is erect with a wary look on his face as he glances over his shoulder. The eight firmly planted wands at his back symbolize that his ideals have held strong and true. They may also symbolize his stalwarts who have stood behind him through the battles along the way. The bandage around his head indicates the wounds of hard blows, but he is without a doubt far from defeat. Yet in his eye is the determination to overcome all odds no matter what it takes. He is standing on higher ground, on a smooth, steady foundation. There is no evidence of emotional overreacting or diverging thoughts. Beyond this fence of wooden wands is a pristine and peaceful landscape of verdant green hills and endless blue skies.

Those who fall under the influence of The Nine of Wands should stay true to their beliefs and convictions and bring out their inner strength and courage. Spiders in our home teach us a great spiritual lesson. Every time we clean up the cobwebs in our house, they do not complain or bite us out of anger like honey bees. They continue to rebuild their web with patience and hard work no matter how many times we rip them off. Though the natives may feel overwhelmed by the mundane hindrances, they will achieve your goals if these people remain determined and bounce back enthusiastically after setbacks. They may have to go alone for a time being, but stay on purpose. These people should heed caution as recklessness could lead to the possibility of harm physically, spiritually or emotionally.

If you think you're beaten.... If you think you're beaten, you are,If you think you dare not, you don't.

If you'd like to win, but think you can't, It's almost for sure, you won't.

If you think you're losing, you've lost. For out in the world we find - Success begins with a person's will,

It's all in the state of mind.

If you think you're outclassed, you are, You've got to think high to rise.

You have to stay with it,

In order to win the prize.

Life's battles don't always go,

To the one with the better plan.

For more often than not, you will win, If only you think you can.

—Kristone

Solomon

Name Number 31

King Solomon of the Kingdom of Israel was great in wisdom, wealth, and power. In the Qur'an, he is a prophet known as Sulaiman, who first constructed a temple in Jerusalem. In one account, known as the Judgment of Solomon, two women came before Solomon to resolve a quarrel over which was the true mother of a baby. When Solomon suggests dividing the living child in two with a sword, the true mother is revealed to him as she is willing to give up her child rather than see the baby killed. Solomon then declares the woman who shows compassion to be the true mother, and gives the baby to her.

Humayun

Name Number 31

Humayun was the second Mughal Emperor who ruled present day Afghanistan, Pakistan, and parts of northern India. He was bitterly betrayed by his four brothers on several occasions and lost his empire for 15 years. He is one emperor who has seen everything from riches to rags. He eventually regained his lost kingdom with Persian aid. On the eve of his death, the Mughal Empire spanned almost one million square kilometers. Interestingly, Humayun was also deeply fascinated by Astrology and the Occult. Upon his accession as emperor, he began to reorganize the administration upon mystically determined principles. The public offices were divided into four distinct groups, for the four elements. The department of Earth was to be in charge of Agriculture and the agricultural sciences, Fire was to be in charge of the Military, Water was the department of the Canals and waterways while Air seemed to have responsibility for everything else.

TEN OF WANDS

You have been given absolute power to bind and to loose, but the I greater the power, the more terrible its responsibility."

-by Fyodor Dostoyevsky

This is exact essence of the Ten of Wands. The card is illustrated by a man holding ten wands with his hands. Those who fall under the influence of this card are bestowed with good opportunities and authority positions in career to gain long lasting fame. Number 32 is ruled by freedom loving Mercury that avoids accountability. However, the native has to learn to bear a great load of responsibility besides enjoying the high status. The Ten of Wands is a magical number that promises international acclaim, good marriage and a fulfilling life.

Aryabhata

Name Number 32

Aryabhata was the first in the line of great mathematician-astronomers from the classical age of Indian mathematics and astronomy. French mathematician Georges Ifrah explains that knowledge of zero was implicit in Aryabhata's place-value system as a place holder for the powers of ten with null coefficients. Aryabhata worked on the approximation for pi (n) which is accurate to five significant figures. He also calculated the area of a triangle using trigonometry. He contributed a lot in the field of astronomy. India's first satellite Aryabhata and the lunar crater Aryabhata are named in his honor.

Ayn Rand

Name Number 32

Ayn Rand was a Russian-American novelist, philosopher, playwright, and screenwriter. She is known for her two best-selling novels and for developing a philosophical system she called Objectivism. She first achieved fame with her novel The Fountainhead, followed by her best- known work, the philosophical novel Atlas Shrugged. She considered reason to be the only means of acquiring knowledge and the most important aspect of her philosophy, stating, "The individual must exist for his own sake, neither sacrificing himself to others nor sacrificing others to himself." Rand has been cited by numerous writers, artists, philosophers, economists, political writers, psychologists and commentators as a profound influence on their lives and thought.

Barack Obama

Name Number 32

Barack Obama is the first African American President of the United States of America and Nobel Peace Prize laureate. Obama was born on 4th August, 1961. His birth date August 4th makes him a Leo highly attractive because of their engaging personality. These individuals are highly rebellious and may have a hard time fitting into a conventional mold. They prefer to do things their own way, even if this means hurting their chances for receiving accolades.

During his term as the President of USA, he has been facing several challenges like economy meltdown, unemployment, health care reforms in the country, war against terrorism in Iraq and Afghanistan, Hunt for Osama bin Laden, crises in Libya and Israel. Time magazine named Barack Obama as its 'Person of the Year' 08 for his historic candidacy and election, which it

described as "the steady march of

seemingly impossible accomplishments".

PAGE OF WANDS

The Page of Wands is symbolized by a young man in royal attire, standing alone in the midst of a barren landscape, talking out loud of his dreams and desires. He holds his wand in a posture of selfconfidence. His robes bear the sign of the salamander, symbolizing the element of Fire. The astrological sign for the Page of Wands is Sagittarius. Under the influence of this master number, the native is goal- oriented, optimistic, daring, attractive, clever, enthusiastic, outspoken but tactless and restless. They are enthusiastic about jump starting things. However these people should make sure that they complete the endeavors come what may. Passion is another quality recommended by the Page of Wands, and this card represents getting your blood flowing. 33 is a combination of two threes. Three communicates and expresses. Multiplied by the 11, it is expressed with style, artistry, and imagination clothed in beauty, love, and harmony. Because 3 uses words with flair, it is no coincidence that this vibration is often found in the charts of famous musicians, singers, actors, and comedians, athletes, politicians, students, teachers and inventors. In the highest octave of it is vibration, The Page of Wands symbolizes the principle of guidance. When expressed to the fullest, it all personal ambition, and instead focuses its considerable abilities toward the spiritual uplifting of mankind. What makes the natives especially impressive is the high level of sincere devotion. This is shown in their determination to seek understanding and wisdom before preaching to others. In its lowest octave, the 33/6 vibration can be manifested as pure lust. Love is chaste and pure that harmonizes and uplifts, heals and regenerates. Whereas lust disharmonizes and degrades wounds and destroys the pure essence of the spirit. Some natives may also feel that they are victims and have been used as doormats by others and prone to ill health as well.

A.P.J.Abdul Kalam

Name Number 33

A.PJ Abdul Kalam is an Aerospace engineer, professor, and chancellor of the Indian Institute of Space Science and Technology (IIST), who served as the 11th President of India. During his term as President, he was popularly known as the People's President. He was awarded the Bharat Ratna, India's highest civilian honor. Before his term as India's president, he worked as an aeronautical engineer and is popularly known as the Missile Man of India for his work on development of ballistic missile and space rocket technology. Kalam played a pivotal organizational, technical and political role in India's nuclear tests. Dr. Kalam launched his mission for the youth of the nation called the What Can I Give Movement. Dr. Kalam also has special interest in the field of arts like writing Tamil poems, and also playing the musical instrument Veena.

Bill Gates

Name Number 33

Bill Gates is an American business magnate, philanthropist, author and chairman of Microsoft. Gates is one of the best-known entrepreneurs of the personal computer revolution. He is consistently ranked among the world's wealthiest people.

Chapter 19: The Cosmic Clock Of Scorpio

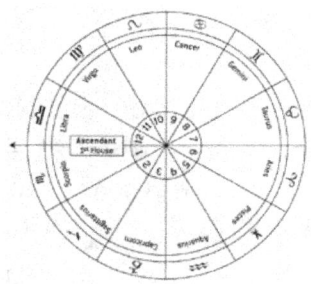

The role of the Cosmic Clock is to show the monthly position of the sun in the Zodiac and its influence expected for Scorpio. For example: A Scorpio who experiences a surge of sexual excitement in June will find that the reason for this is the sun in Gemini, his 8th house. However, a slowdown in energy is expected for August, when the sun moves into Leo, the 10th house.

The Monthly Forecast

Scorpio

Sagittarius   Capricorn   Aquarius   Pisces

Aries
Taurus
Gemini
Cancer
Leo
Virgo
Libra
October 23 – November 21
November 22 – December 20
December 21 – January 20
January 21 – February 19
February 19 – March 20
March 21 – April 19
April 20 – May 20
May 21 – June 20
June 21 – July 22
July 23 – August 22
August 23 – September 22
September 23 – October 22

Sun in the 1st house
Sun in the 2nd house
Sun in the 3rd house
Sun in the 4th house
Sun in the 5th house
Sun in the 6th house
Sun in the 7th house
Sun in the 8th house
Sun in the 9th house
Sun in the 10th house
Sun in the 11th house
Sun in the 12th house

Note: For characteristics and meanings of the 12 houses of the Cosmic Clock, see chapter on the monthly forecast.

Scorpio: Relationships with Other Signs

Scorpio 1st house Sagittarius 2nd house Capricorn 3rd house Aquarius 4th house Pisces 5th house Aries 6th house Taurus 7th house Gemini 8th house Cancer 9th house Leo 10th house Virgo 11th house Libra 12th house

Example: A Scorpio man will experience detachment from a Virgo woman but will find it difficult to separate from a Libra.

SAGITTARIUS – NOVEMBER 22nd to DECEMBER 20th

Sagittarius is linked in astrology to aspects of thought, to feelings of liberty, justice, and freedom, and to symbols of mobility, adventure, and autonomy. There is also a connection to institutes of higher learning, sports, legal enterprises, nature, and animals, especially horses.

Sagittarius usually counsels others and has an air of arrogance or aristocracy. Intuition is excellent. He is outwardly candid, rebellious, and provocative but also quite diplomatic.

Space is perceived as a value in its own right. Physical as well as intellectual space is symbolized in the form of the Centaur as half man and half horse. These two parts express the physical and primal side of Sagittarius, while the arrow symbolizes the shot into the far distance, not only in a geographical sense but also in the search for spiritual and philosophical meaning of life. This is reflected mainly in the asking of questions, which interest Sagittarius more than the answers.

From the political point of view, and in connection with the subject of freedom, we can use Winston Churchill as an example. He fought against the Germans in World War II and was determined to win at any price. He was also known for his famous Sagittarius-like statement: "You don't cross an abyss with two steps but rather a leap." Sagittarius knows how to speculate and gamble; this is something hidden deep inside his nature. Another Sagittarius, Frank Sinatra, fulfilled this in Las Vegas and also sang, "I did it my way...." – the Sagittarius way.

Sagittarius has a problem with the religious establishment. He can be a theologian however not orthodox. Left-wing Israeli parliament member Shulamit Aloni has always had trouble with the religious parties, and for many years she has fought for liberty, justice, and equality as a courageous Sagittarius. Sinead O'Connor, another well-known Sagittarius, abhors Catholicism and in one of her performances even tore up a picture of the Pope. Former Tel Aviv mayor Ronny Milo was unable to identify with the religious right of Israel and like a true Sagittarius formed his own political party.

As far from religion as east is from west are actresses Jane Fonda and Kim Basinger. Fonda, a provocative Sagittarius in life as well as in film, was born on a horse ranch, and appeared at the age of 16 at school wearing nothing but high heels and a string of pearls. Fonda provoked a great deal of controversy with her visit to Hanoi during the Vietnam War and her radical political views. Years later, she successfully marketed books and videotapes of her personal exercise routines. Kim Basinger is known as a sex symbol, starring in such movies as "9 ½ Weeks."

Sagittarius is connected in nature to the tiger and the wild cat. Tigers "do it" during the mating season nearly 300 times a day. A close relative, the jaguar, is the symbol of aristocracy on the luxury British car. One provocative Sagittarius was Jim Morrison, lead vocalist of "The Doors," who dropped his pants and masturbated on stage during a performance in 1969, while crying, "Is this enough for you?" There is something daring, rude, and brazen about the enormous wish for freedom. An additional Sagittarius from the music archives is Jimi Hendrix. Another

Sagittarius, Alexander Solzhenitsyn, was the only free man in Soviet Russia – or at least the only one who allowed himself to say what nobody else would dare. Solzhenitsyn is the embodiment of Sagittarius in the spirit of political freedom. Kirk Douglas, a Sagittarius who rode many horses in Western films, is known to read the Bible and be interested in religion during his golden years. In my opinion, more than anyone else, Mark Twain, the author of "Tom Sawyer and Huckleberry Finn" represents Sagittarius. The questions of liberty, freedom, and justice are the central motives in Huck's indecision as to whether or not to assist Jim to escape or to turn him in to the white American establishment. Huck decides to help the slave, thus making a significant Sagittarian choice of justice according to one's inner conscience.

Brad Pitt is also Sagittarius and searched for spiritual enlightenment for "Seven Years in Tibet."

Conception of Time – Capricorn is located in the 2nd house, which connects time directly with money and possessions. Sagittarius is a stickler for time as he sees it, and from Virgo in the 10th house comes the punctuality and exactitude in connection with work. He is critical of the lateness of others, but he could also absorb some criticism himself. Time is production and purpose, and the view is most realistic.

Career and Work – Despite the natural inclination toward open spaces for ideas and big talk, many Sagittarians work in fields that require attention to detail and exactitude, such as medicine, teaching, and therapeutic services. The critical dimension comes from Virgo, which occupies the 10th house of careers, and Sagittarius will absorb criticism, something that is not acceptable and not especially liked.

Taurus in the 6th house could indicate a profession associated with agriculture, land, banking, finance, or real estate.

There is a desire for stability and routine, which does not exactly match the characteristic natural mobility of the Sagittarius archetype. Import-export, gambling, nature and animals (including horse ranching), hotels and tourism, management, publishing, communications, and therapeutic professions are also connected with Sagittarius.

Money – There is conflict between the speculative nature of Sagittarius and the location of Capricorn in the 2nd house, which points to a serious and careful attitude toward money rather than that of squandering. Money is connected to gradual and hard work, to adult images, and to the utilization of authority gained with time. Cancer in the 8th house as well as Capricorn in the 2nd indicates a connection between money and family, and there could be inheritance related in some way to the mother image. Sagittarius develops slowly and will experience periods of financial limitation or a fatalistic sense in connection with this. Scorpio in the 12th house could lead to financial losses as a result of hidden enemies, fraud, or manipulation.

Relationships – There could be sudden and surprising love relationships and the possibility of connections during a flight, through a computer or the media, or at a social event. The fact that Libra occupies the 11th house, quantum in essence, injects a dimension of anti-linear, inconsistency, and fragmentation in the area of relationships and marriage. However, this disturbance in rhythm enables relationships based on space and friendship and could be the condition for marriage and partnership with a Sagittarius. There could also be a connection to travel abroad and studies.

Sudden separations from partners can occur, as well as surprising and unconventional relationships. The partner could be tall, intelligent and communicative, due to Gemini's position in the 7th house, a situation that also is related to duality and can indicate more than one marriage.

Good verbal communication is a necessary condition for marriage. For Sagittarius women, Aries in the 5th house indicates a male figure worthy of prizes who can be proud of her. There could be young love and romance as well as a famous partner or one connected with management.

Conclusion

Thanks for making it through to the end of this book. Let's hope it was informative and able to provide you with all of the tools you need to achieve your goals whatever they may be.

It is worth remembering that true numerology is sacred. Although this may be hard to notice in our modern age, the truth remains that it is a sacred science and art. Also, if you are serious about pursuing this ancient study, you must develop a good soul and a kind heart. After all, the closer you are to divinity, the easier it will be for you to hear the voice of the Divine.

The next step is to apply everything that you have learned about numerology in your day-to-day living. It is time for you to live in harmony with the numbers and be the master of your life.

www.ingramcontent.com/pod-product-compliance
Lightning Source LLC
Chambersburg PA
CBHW072001070526
44583CB00015B/1287